BEAD METAMORPHOSIS

**EXQUISITE
JEWELRY
FROM CUSTOM
COMPONENTS**

LISA KAN

INTERWEAVE.
interweave.com

Editor
Michelle Mach

Technical Editor
Bonnie Brooks

Copy Editor
Karen Levy

Art Direction
Julia Boyles and Charlene Tiedemann

Photography
Joe Coca

Photo Styling
Ann Sabin Swanson

Illustrations
Bonnie Brooks

Cover + Interior Design
Pamela Norman

Production
Katherine Jackson

Interweave
A division of F+W Media, Inc.
4868 Innovation Dr.
Fort Collins, CO 80525
interweave.com

Manufactured in the United States by RR Donnelley Roanoke

Library of Congress Cataloging-in-Publication Data

Kan, Lisa.
Bead metamorphosis : exquisite jewelry from custom components / LisaKan.
    pages cm
ISBN 978-1-59668-825-4 (pbk.)
ISBN 978-1-59668-826-1 (PDF)
1. Jewelry making. 2. Beadwork.
I. Title.
TT212.K359 2014
745.594'2--dc23
2014028517

10 9 8 7 6 5 4 3 2 1

ACKNOWLEDGMENTS

There are not enough words I can write to express my thanks and love to Nicholas, my wonderfully supportive husband, who has always been the man behind the scenes, the Bead Show Roadie (BSR), and the strength that I seek in challenging moments to lift me back up—in sickness and in health. He made the BEST chicken noodle soup while I was sick several times during the writing of this book.

To Allison Korleski, who I affectionately call the "stalker that I welcome," who was patient to wait three years for me to find the time to write and develop the ideas for *Bead Metamorphosis*. An idea is just an idea unless put into motion. Thank you for being the "F"orce in my F=ma. I appreciate the freedom to express my vision and to challenge beaders in the projects of this book.

Most dear to me are my two editors, Michelle Mach and Bonnie Brooks. Michelle kept me on track and helped work around my busy exhibit schedule. Her fine skills as an editor are apparent through these pages. And, there is no one else I would rather work with than Bonnie Brooks as my technical editor and illustrator. Bonnie is the reason why my diagrams flow so well with the text instructions. These two expert editors make me sound and look good! *Bead Metamorphosis* is as much their book as it is mine.

This book would not be a book without the talented and hardworking Interweave staff, especially Joe Coca, Karen Levy, Kerry Jackson, Hollie Hill, Pamela Norman, and Ann Swanson.

I also want to give thanks to my sisters Sandy and Tina Kan, Melinda Barta, Marlene Blessing, the Starmans (Jerry, Nichole, and Dave), Heather Patterson-Ogden, Hynek Strnad, Nir Kronenberg, Martin Bonaventre, Linda "Polly" Kanazaki, and especially Glennis Dolce. Because of your inspiration and friendship or help in other areas of my bead world, I was able to focus on composing this book.

Last and most importantly, no one is more deserving of my thanks than all my customers, my fellow beaders, and my "students" who year after year asked me, "So when are you writing a new book?"

There is always a perfect time to take on a huge project like writing a book. In between *Bead Romantique* and *Bead Metamorphosis*, life happened! A book project generally takes up a year. That's many long days and nights, from concept to inception, designing and then creating, researching and procuring the right components for that perfect design, scheduling and meeting deadlines, sacrificing sleep, holidays, and family time, etc. In the end, it is all well worth the sacrifices. The last year, 2013, was the perfect time.

I always like to keep my projects under wraps until they are completed and to keep everyone on their toes guessing. I know you've all waited a long time for the sequel to *Bead Romantique*. I hope to continue teaching and sharing my design concepts through my writing, reaching more beaders than I could ever in a classroom setting. Thank you for being in my bead world.

For Audrey,
Kayla, and Wesley—
the next generation
of artists.
Love,
Auntie Lisa

CONTENTS

6 From Butterflies & Dragonflies to Beads

8 Materials & Tools

14 Tips & Tricks

16 Deco Chandelier Earrings

20 Deco Lace Bracelet

26 Isadora Earrings

32 Audrey Fringe Bracelet

40 Rivoli Scallop Chain Earrings

44 Chrysanthemum Brooch

50 Sundara Necklace

62 Kayla Lariat

74 Trefoil Earrings

80 Catherine Bracelet

86 Catherine Necklace

98 Crown Jewels Earrings

102 Bella Fiore

110 Hanami

118 Crown Jewels Necklace

130 Encanto Necklace

142 Color & Inspiration

150 Basic Techniques

158 Project Resources

159 Where to Shop

160 Index

FROM BUTTERFLIES & DRAGONFLIES TO BEADS

If you are not already familiar with my design style from my first book, *Bead Romantique*, my beadwork is often inspired by different historical periods. I have to confess that as I began designing projects for B*ead Metamorphosis*, I spent a lot of time also catching up watching *The Tudors* and two seasons of *Game of Thrones*.

Seeing all the costumes and jewelry from the respective periods inspired me to create designs like the Catherine Collection, the Crown Jewels Collection, and Sundara. My fondness for the art nouveau, art deco, and Roaring Twenties periods resulted in the Deco Lace Collection, Isadora Earrings, and the Audrey Fringe Bracelet. Mother Nature is also close to my heart and came to life through Bella Fiore, Hanami, the Chrysanthemum Brooch, and the Kayla Lariat. The metamorphosis theme, central to this book, is best illustrated in the design Encanto, where you can disassemble and reassemble components that are both reversible as well as interchangeable.

All the designs in *Bead Metamorphosis* are broken down into easy-to-follow steps and diagrams. Designs in collections have similar components that transform through a change of beads, bead counts, or methods of embellishment. Like the wondrous transformation of a butterfly or dragonfly in nature, each component transforms to create many variations. As you progress through the projects, I hope they inspire you to think about modular and component designing.

I also focused on creating wearable jewelry with innovative, modern shaped beads such as SuperDuos, Rizos, Rullas, and CzechMate bricks and lentils, all of which can be easily found at your local bead shop or online.

In the Color and Inspiration chapter, I share how I develop my ideas for my designs. I approach color in a non-academic manner with everyday objects and observations. Inspiration is all around us—you really don't have to look that hard—and eventually choosing colors for your projects will be a natural instinct.

Beadweaving is not an instant-gratification craft. It is an art that builds on the simple skills first and then develops into more intricate beadwork with layers upon layers of personal creativity. I enjoy building on the standard stitches, resulting in a design that appears complex but is created using simple techniques, therefore showing endless possibilities of each stitch. It is vital to learn the basic bead stitches: peyote, brick, square, ladder, right-angle weave, herringbone (Ndebele), netting, and others that will develop skills for more complicated stitches such as St. Petersburg and cubic right-angle weave.

When and if you do get stuck with any of the projects, I am only an email away at LisaKanDesigns@yahoo.com.

Enjoy and bead creatively,

Lisa

MATERIALS & TOOLS

Those who find beadweaving rewarding know that selecting materials and colors are two of the most important factors in creating beautiful results. With the amount of hours one puts into weaving tiny beads into cohesive designs, it is key to start with a selection of quality materials and the proper tools.

Never hurry or rush to finish a project. A design should look as beautiful in the back as it does in the front. Taking shortcuts in finishing techniques will only result in an unsatisfactory outcome.

BEAD SELECTION

↓ Seed Beads

Seed beads come in a variety of sizes. The size is indicated by a number; the smaller the numbered size (6°, 8°, 10°, 11°, 13°, 15°, etc.), the larger the bead. The seed beads

used throughout this book are all Japanese seed beads, mostly the round shape in various colors and finishes. Miyuki, Toho, and Matsuno are the three major manufacturers of Japanese seed beads. Toho beads have the largest holes of the three companies, making them great for designs that have multiple thread passes. Some seed bead colors (with different color nomenclature) cross over among the three manufacturers and therefore can be used interchangeably.

Seed bead finishes and manufacturing processes have improved since I wrote *Bead Romantique*. In the past, I avoided galvanized seed beads. Both Toho and Miyuki now produce "Permanent Finish" and "Duracoat" seed beads, respectively, which are less prone to rub off and deteriorate. Also, with the collaboration between the Japanese seed bead manufacturers and Czech bead manufacturers, additional colors are now available with aftermarket coatings such as Picasso, travertine, hematite, magic, capri gold, sliperit, and vega. Even now, I personally avoid dyed seed beads because they tend to fade over time with wear.

Crystals, Pearls, and Shaped Beads

Rivolis and **Fancy Stones** are multifaceted stones made by Swarovski that are used as cabochons and bezel set with seed beads. The projects in this book use size 12mm, 14mm, and 16mm rivolis and pear-shaped rhinestones. Most of the rhinestones are foil-backed to enhance color and sparkle. There are also a variety of after-market custom coatings and effects applied by EH Ashley on Swarovski components that add color dimension to beadwork. Some of these beautiful coatings are Purple Haze, Chili Pepper, Verde, Brandy, Sahara, Sphinx, Champagne, and Glacier Blue. (For a full list, visit EHashley.com.)

Crystal pearls and **Czech glass pearls** are produced by Swarovski and Czech bead manufacturers. Crystal pearls are crystals coated with a thick pearl-like substance. They come in various sizes and shapes. The number of coatings determines its durability. The coatings on both crystal and glass pearls can be scratched off from high abrasion or friction. Simulated imitation glass pearls have the look of genuine pearls, but are uniform and economical.

Czech Shaped Innovations and two-hole beads are used in the designs of this book. The Czech Republic, well known for its glass beads and special coatings, has been quite innovative in introducing and expanding the two-hole bead selection. Some designs in this book use beads such as SuperDuos, Rullas, and the CzechMate System from Starman, Inc., to create historically inspired designs with modern components. These Czech glass beads are pressed with a mold, resulting in a uniform shape for precision beadwork. Everything fits together like a puzzle. Other shaped beads like the Rizo drops are also pressed glass. They make wonderful accents or embellishments. There is never a loss of choices, as all these beads are available in similar color palettes. The question is which color and shape to use!

FINDINGS

Tube clasps used in the projects are a seamless way to finish a design that does not disrupt its flow. The tube clasp contains two parts, one slightly bigger than the other, which slide and lock into place with friction, one inside the other.

↓ Snaps are an economical way to create custom hidden closures. Because there is a female and a male portion to the clasp, it is necessary to make sure that the correct sides meet when attaching them. I generally like to use the 3/0 size and hide the snaps inconspicuously behind beadwork.

{ COLOR COMBINATIONS }

Knowing how to select colors and mixing colors for a harmonious palette is a challenge for most beginner beaders. It is even a challenge for a seasoned beader. As your beading experience grows, you will find favorite color combinations to add to your repertoire. The Color and Inspiration chapter (page 142) discusses this topic in more depth.

↑ Blending matte with shiny or transparent with opaque beads can create subtle "visual" textures. Beads such as Swarovski crystals, Czech fire-polished beads, freshwater or glass pearls, shaped seed beads, or shaped Czech two-hole pressed-glass beads add interest to a design. Vintage beads, antique buttons, or an old brooch can also bring an Old-World feel to contemporary designs. I tend to use muted and subdued colors to instill a vintage feel. Remember that beads and your beadwork may change in color based on the nearby beads and even the thread you use.

Chain used in the projects is the finest size that can incorporate several thread passes with 6 lb FireLine. Chain adds movement to designs with little effort. Because the chain is being stitched to beadwork it is important to use chain with soldered rings. This does mean that there will be some waste when cutting chain.

↓ **Earring findings** are important to the overall look. Two of my favorite earring findings are the lever-back and the open ear wire hooks with a 3mm ball. These classy options create streamlined designs that do not take away from the overall beadwork. The flexibility of the open earring hook allows you to interchange earring parts easily with several pairs of earring findings in various metal finishes.

THREAD SELECTION
Thread Color

Thread color is an important consideration in beadwork because it affects the final design color, especially on transparent beads or with stitches that may show the thread, such as right-angle weave. All of the projects in this book utilize 6 lb smoke FireLine, but thread choice is a personal preference. Always try to select thread color to match closely to the beads you are using. If the thread is part of the design, select your contrasting colors carefully.

Thread Types

FireLine is a stiff nylon fishing line that has transitioned into the beading world. It is readily available and cost-effective when purchased from fishing and outdoor-supply companies. This thread comes in several strength tests and is available in crystal clear, smoke, or flame green colors. (Kelley Darcangelo of the Sparkle Spot Bead Shop worked independently with a chemist to create additional FireLine colors, which are available from SparkleSpot.com.) FireLine does not tangle easily, but if it does, knots can be easily removed with an awl. No waxing or conditioning is required. The number of bead passes you make will determine the weight used. I prefer using crystal clear when working with light-colored beads and smoke for darker-colored beads. The smoke FireLine has a tendency to rub off, so be aware that your fingers will start appearing "dirty" as you work. Flatten the ends with your fingernails or chain-nose pliers before threading.

Silamide is a twisted, pre-waxed nylon thread that is available in 100-yard (91.4 m) cards and in 500-yard (457 m) spools in one size (size A). Although there is a limited selection of colors compared to other threads, I prefer it because it does not fray or tear apart when I backtrack to remove stitches. The light brown Silamide is a neutral color that blends well with most beadwork and is my favorite color. Furthermore, you only need to condition this thread by pre-stretching before beading because it is pre-waxed. Beeswax or Thread Heaven is only used on the ends before threading. Be aware that the ends of crystals have sharp edges that will cut through Silamide over time.

One-G thread is manufactured by the Toho Bead Company. It is a nylon thread similar to Nymo (size B), but is much stronger and less likely to fray. It is silky and smooth to the touch. The sand ash color is similar to the Silamide light brown and works with most beadwork. I don't use thread conditioner often, but it is useful to have some on hand if you find it difficult to thread your needles. One-G has become one of my favorite beading threads.

Because I am a tight beadweaver, the general rule I follow is that if there are Swarovski crystals (which have sharp edges that may cut your thread) or if I want a more structured finished design, I use FireLine. If I desire more drape and flow, where the beads used will not damage the thread, then I select One-G and/or Silamide. Many beaders also like using KO thread, Nymo, C-Lon, DandyLine, or PowerPro. I predominately use FireLine, and I generally do not use a thread conditioner.

NEEDLE SELECTION

There are as many different types of beading needles (long, short, sharp, etc.) as there are brands to select from. Nearly all of the projects specify size 12 beading needles. The larger the number in needle size, the thinner the needle and the smaller the eye. Size 12 needles are the staple for me, but if you are more comfortable with a larger size needle, the Tulip size 11 is an all-around go-to size for beadwork with fewer passes. As with thread selection, needle selection is a personal preference.

Tulip beading needles have revolutionized the way beaders weave. These innovative needles are flexible, super-thin, springy, and strong. They resist bending and breakage to last longer than other beading needles. After I was introduced to these beading needles in mid-2011, I have not used any other brand of needle, as the Tulips last through many hours of beading. The tip of the needle is slightly rounded to avoid splitting the thread. The eye of the needle is gold-plated to make threading easier, as there are no burrs like you might experience on other needles. I keep a size 13 needle in my stash because there may be times I need to switch to a size 13 for tight spots.

TOOLS

→ **Round-** and **chain-nose pliers** are indispensable for your toolbox. I prefer using Japanese ultra-small precision pliers made for electronic work, because most of the wirework in the book uses 24-gauge wire. As with beads, do not skimp on your tools because they are the extension of your hands. Good tools create a more finished look to your design. Chain-nose pliers come in handy for beadwork to straighten bent needles or to pull needles through a tight spot. I also like to finish my wrapped loops by using ultrafine chain-nose pliers to tuck in the ends of the wire.

→ **Flush wire cutters** are required to ensure that your wired projects have a finished look. Most stainless steel flush wire cutters are meant to cut nonferrous metals (gold, gold-filled, fine silver, sterling silver, copper, and brass). A stainless steel flush wire cutter is not for cutting stainless steel beading and/or memory wires. Using your cutters to cut stainless materials will create divots and damage the cutter's blade. There are designated wire cutters for stainless steel products. Using economical or inexpensive cutters will pinch the wire ends and do not create a nice flush cut, which will be visible.

TIP

As with beads, do not skimp on your tools because they are the extension of your hands.

A **beading awl** is another indispensable tool. Besides beading needles, the Tulip Company also manufacturers a fine beading awl that has a thin, sharp tip perfect for making small holes or deburring pearl beads. An awl is used to reposition a small seed bead (such as a size 15°) for easier access to the needle. It is also useful for removing an unwanted seed bead from the beadwork without damaging or cutting the thread. You can also easily tease knots open.

Scissors such as children's Fiskars that are sharp and of good quality are a must. A clean cut will also mean an easier time threading your needles!

A Berkley thread and fishing line cutter called the **Hot Line Cutter** comes in handy to burn the ends of thread to avoid fraying. The Berkley cutter is more economic than the Thread Zapper, which is actually a tool, adapted from wax carving. The Berkley cutter also comes with an extra tip. Some beaders use a lighter, but those are a bit tricky to handle and require a steady hand. You don't want to accidentally burn your beadwork after all your hard work.

TIP

A task lamp that emulates daylight is very important to help you distinguish the true color of your beads.

Beading pads are very helpful for keeping track of beads and needles. I use a velvet jewelry pad with a stiff cardboard interior wrapped in foam. This surface makes it easier to pick up beads and also provides a place to pin extra needles while I work. I place the pad inside a jewelry display tray so beads do not accidentally roll around and make a big mess. You can find these at jewelry supply houses. There are fancier beading boards and travel cases you may want to invest in, but this is an effective and economical solution that works perfectly well.

An **OttLite or task lamp** that emulates daylight (about a 5,000 Kelvin rating) is very important to help you distinguish the true color of your beads.

No-Tangle bobbins are great when using longer lengths of FireLine or if I am creating a rope or designing beadwork that can be beaded from both directions. I start beading from the center of the FireLine length after spooling half onto the bobbin. You can also use a thread card for the same purpose. Some beaders also use a sticky note by wrapping the thread around and folding the sticky note along the adhesive side to secure temporarily.

A **rotary cutter** is indispensable for cutting straight edges in fabric, leather, or paper when used with a ruler on a self-healing mat. A self-healing mat protects your work surface from damage. Olfa is the brand I prefer for both, but there are many similar products available.

A **bracelet gauge** is not necessary, but makes it easy to measure your wrist, especially for bangle designs. The gauge is generally made of steel and has ½" (1.3 cm) incremental slots. Fit the bracelet gauge into a slot and make sure the ring can easily slide on and off your wrist. In the absence of a bracelet gauge, a ruler or tape measure and a strip of paper will serve the same function.

TIPS & TRICKS

↓ MAKING SAMPLES

When making a large design, make a small sample first to evaluate the color harmony and balance before moving forward. More than likely, if you don't like the way the sample looks, you won't like it in a larger piece. I love modular component design because there is a small amount of time invested before you fully delve in. Because components are added as you go, it is easy to stop and start your beadwork. I have been known to cut up beadwork and start over. Don't fear those words "start over." It is much better than saying "I dislike my design" after hours of work.

STOP OR TENSION BEADS

Although a majority of the projects do not mention the use of a stop bead, if you find it difficult to hold your beadwork when initially stringing beads, you can use a stop bead to hold it in place. Use a bead that is a different color or larger than those in your beadwork design so you can easily spot it later for removal. To add a stop bead, string a bead and pass through it twice more, leaving an appropriate tail length for your project. Be careful not to split the thread on the second pass (this can happen even if you are using FireLine), so that the bead will slide off easily when you are ready to remove it. Remember to take out the stop bead before continuing!

HOLDING YOUR BEADWORK

The way you hold your beadwork and the direction in which you bead will determine the beadwork tension. Tension is very important, and with practice you will find a happy medium. I have a tendency of being a tight beadweaver. I hold my work on my left hand between my thumb and forefinger, beading with my right hand. When I am doing a complex connection that requires thread tension, I sometimes wrap the working thread around my right forefinger several times.

THREAD LENGTHS

I use one to two wingspans of a single length of thread for most bead starts. This is the most comfortable length for me to avoid knots and tangles. I rarely use double thread, as I find it difficult to undo if you make an error and have to backtrack. I use longer thread if I am creating a rope or have a design that can be beaded in multiple directions. Those are the times I incorporate a No-Tangle bobbin and roll up half of the length to avoid having to reconnect new thread too often. I like beading efficiency! Some beaders prefer shorter lengths for faster beading. Use the length that is comfortable for you; the suggested lengths in the projects are not set in stone.

ADDING NEW THREAD

When beading an elaborate project, you will invariably run out of thread. The technique for adding thread depends on the bead stitch. Most often, when you have about 4" (10.2 cm) remaining of the working thread, weave about 1" (2.5 cm) into several beads with the new thread. Leaving a 2" to 3" (5 to 7.5 cm) tail, pass under the thread from a previous thread pass and make a half-hitch knot. Follow the thread path of the stitch and repeat with a second knot. Weave to the location of the original thread and continue beading with the new thread. Weave the old thread into the newly beaded stitches by repeating a half-hitch knot through several beads later, twice.

In flat or cubic right-angle weave, you can just weave through the beads looping around to secure the new thread. Tying a half-hitch knot may show in right-angle-weave corners. Thread can be added in many ways as long as it does not show and is secured; it doesn't matter which method you adopt.

TURNING

A quick way to turn the weaving direction is to pass under the thread from a previous thread pass and make a half-hitch knot. Then weave back toward the direction you want. Keep in mind to always follow the thread path of whatever stitch you are using so that no thread shows.

FINISHING

To finish the ends of your beadwork, different threads require different treatments. Some beaders weave the tail thread through several beads again and again and then just trim. However, most of the time (except with right-angle-weave patterns), I generally make at least two or three half-hitch knots between several beads at each interval before I trim. With FireLine, you can often make a flush cut close to the beadwork without further treatment or use a thread burner to cauterize the ends into a small ball. If you are using Silamide or One-G, cut close to the beadwork and add a dab of clear nail polish to the ends to prevent fraying.

↓ FRAY CHECK

It is not necessary and not effective to use fray check on silk ribbon or shibori silk satin ribbons, as it will discolor the fabric. Frayed edges are part of the charm of using hand-dyed ribbons, as shown by the designs in this book. Ribbons can be folded or stitched to cover the unfinished edges. Both ribbons used in the book are bias cut, meaning that long strips of silk fabric are cut at an angle and then joined together to form a continuous length.

TECHNIQUES

Right-angle weave

Wrapped loop

MATERIALS

0.25 g lavender blue gold luster 11° Japanese seed beads (A)

0.25 g bronze 11° Japanese seed beads (B)

0.5 g bronze 15° Japanese seed beads (C)

4 gold matte 3×6mm Czech 2-hole bricks

10 blue zircon 3mm crystal bicones

2 cream rose 4mm crystal pearls

2" (5 cm) of gold-filled 24-gauge wire

12" (30.5 cm) of gold-filled 2.25mm flat cable chain

2 gold-filled ear wires with 3mm ball

Smoke 6 lb braided beading thread

TOOLS

Size 12 beading needles

Round-nose pliers

Chain-nose pliers

Wire cutters

Ruler

Scissors

SIZE

3" (7.5 cm)

LEVEL

Beginner

DECO CHANDELIER

EARRINGS

Without all the frills of lace found in the Deco Lace Bracelet (page 20), these earrings have a motif of Xs and Os. One of my favorite art historical periods is the art deco period (1930s to 1940s). I utilize chain with a three-tiered effect to allow fun movement as the wearer swings and sways.

1 Prepare and cut the chain for the scallops. *Note: There will be about 1" (2.5 cm) of chain lost due to cutting.* Cut the following lengths: four ½" (1.3 cm), two 1" (2.5 cm), two 1½" (3.8 cm), and two 2" (5 cm). Separate the chain by size and arrange in this order on the work surface.

2 With 15" (38 cm) of thread, string 2A, 1B, 2A, 1B, 2A, 1B, 2A, and 1B. Tie into a ring with a square knot, leaving a 6" (15 cm) tail. Pass through the first 2A **(Fig. 1)**.

3 String 1C, 1 brick, the 1" (2.5 cm) chain, 1C, the 1½" (3.8 cm) chain, 1C, the 2" (5 cm) chain, and 3C. Pass through the other brick hole. String 1C. Pass through the 2A on the ring again. To stiffen and reinforce, pass through all beads and chains added in this step. Pass through the 2A and then through the next B **(Fig. 2)**.

4 String 1 bicone and 1C. Skip the C, then pass back through the bicone and the B again. Pass through the bicone and C once more to stiffen. Pass back through the bicone, the B, and the next 2A **(Fig. 3)**.

5 String 1C, 1 brick, 3C, the opposite end of the 2" (5 cm) chain, 1C, the opposite end of the 1½" (3.8 cm) chain, 1C, and the opposite end of the 1" (2.5 cm) chain. Pass through the other brick hole. String 1C. Pass through the 2A. To stiffen and reinforce, pass through all beads and chains added in this step. Pass through the 2A and the next B.

6 Repeat Step 4 **(Fig. 4)**.

7 String 1C, 1 brick, one ½" (1.3 cm) chain, and 5C. Pass through the other brick hole. String 1C. Pass through the 2A. To stiffen and reinforce, weave back through all beads and the chain added in this step. Pass through 2A and the next B.

8 Repeat Step 4 **(Fig. 5)**.

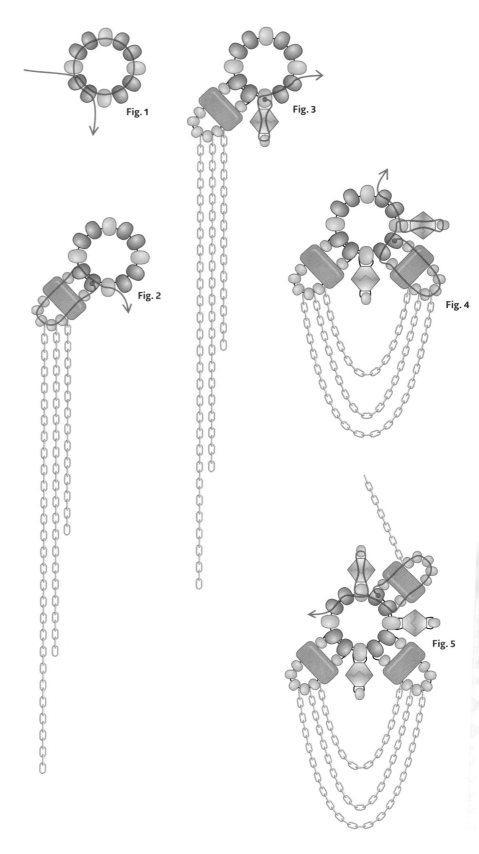

Fig. 1

Fig. 2

Fig. 3

Fig. 4

Fig. 5

Fig. 6

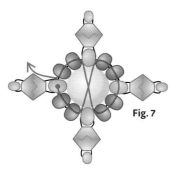

Fig. 7

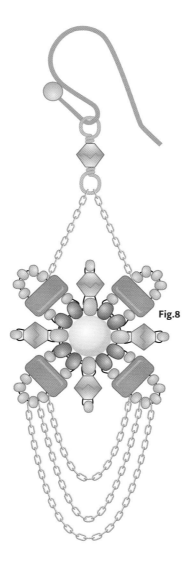

Fig.8

9 String 1C, 1 brick, 5C, and one ½" (1.3 cm) chain. Pass through the other brick hole. String 1C and pass through the 2A. To stiffen and reinforce, pass through all beads and the chain added in this step. Pass through the 2A and the next B.

10 Repeat Step 4 **(Fig. 6)**.

11 String 1 pearl and pass through the opposite-facing 2A in reverse diagonal direction. Pass through 1B and 2A. Pass back through the pearl and through the opposite-facing 2A in reverse diagonal direction. Secure the thread through the original ring from Step 2 and trim **(Fig. 7)**.

12 Create a ¹⁄₁₂" (2 mm) loop with one end of the 2" (5 cm) wire. Insert the left chain and then the right chain. Ensure the chains are not twisted, then complete the wrapped loop. Insert 1 bicone and repeat creating a ¹⁄₁₂" (2 mm) wrapped loop on other end. String the loop through the open loop of 1 ear wire **(Fig. 8)**.

13 Repeat Steps 1–12 to create the other earring.

DECO LACE
BRACELET

TECHNIQUES

Peyote stitch

Two-drop peyote stitch

Right-angle weave

Ladder stitch

Picot

Sewing

MATERIALS

1 g lavender gold luster 11° Japanese seed beads (A)

1 g Montana blue gold luster 11° Japanese seed beads (B)

0.5 g bronze 11° Japanese seed beads (C)

3 g lavender gold luster 15° Japanese seed beads (D)

1.5 g Montana blue gold luster 15° Japanese seed beads (E)

1.25 g bronze 15° Japanese seed beads (F)

7 gold luster 2.5×5mm 2-hole seed beads (G)

7 cream rose 4mm crystal pearls

32 blue zircon 3mm crystal bicones

24 gold matte 3×6mm Czech 2-hole bricks

1 black size 3/0 sew-on snap set

Smoke 6 lb braided beading thread

TOOLS

Size 12 beading needles

Scissors

SIZE

7½" (19 cm)

LEVEL

Intermediate

Floral and lacy quatrefoils are stitched together to create a deco-inspired bracelet with the help of two-hole brick beads. A quatrefoil is an ornamental motif of four overlapping circles often used in the Gothic and Renaissance periods. The hidden snap closure continues the motif and makes the bracelet reversible.

TIPS

→ Although CzechMate 2-hole bricks were used for this project, you can substitute Rullas, SuperDuos, or Preciosa Twin beads for an alternate version.

→ If you do not like using snaps for closures, you can use a two-strand clasp.

→ To prevent the lace edges from curling, reinforce the edge beads to stiffen the beadwork as necessary and flatten before wearing.

MAKING THE COMPONENTS

1 With a 36" (91.5 cm) length of thread, string 2A, 1C, 2A, 1C, 2A, 1C, 2A, and 1C. Join into a ring with a square knot, leaving a 6" (15 cm) tail. Pass through the first 2A **(Fig. 1)**.

2 String 1F, 1 brick, and 5F. Pass through the other brick hole on the same side. String 1F and pass through the 2A and then through the next C **(Fig. 2)**.

3 String 1 bicone and 1F. Skip the F and pass back through the bicone, 1C, and the next 2A **(Fig. 3)**.

4 Repeat Steps 2–3 three times. After the last repeat of Step 3, pass through the first F, the brick and the 3F added in Step 2 **(Fig. 4)**.

5 Use the tail thread to add 1 pearl to the center. Pass through the 2A. String 1 pearl and pass through the opposite-facing 2A in reverse diagonal direction **(Fig. 5, blue thread)**. Pass through 1B and 2A. Pass back through the pearl and through the opposite 2A in reverse diagonal direction. Secure the thread through the original ring and trim. Flip the beadwork over and return to the working thread **(Fig. 5, red thread)**.

6 String 9D and pass through the F above the bicone. String 9D and pass through the third F (or center bead) of the picot above the brick **(Fig. 6)**.

7 Repeat Step 6 three times. After the last repeat, pass through the first D added in Step 6.

8 String 1D, skip 1D, and pass through the third D from Step 6. Repeat three times, weaving 1D into the fifth, seventh, and ninth Ds from Step 6. Pass through the F above the bicone **(Fig. 7)**.

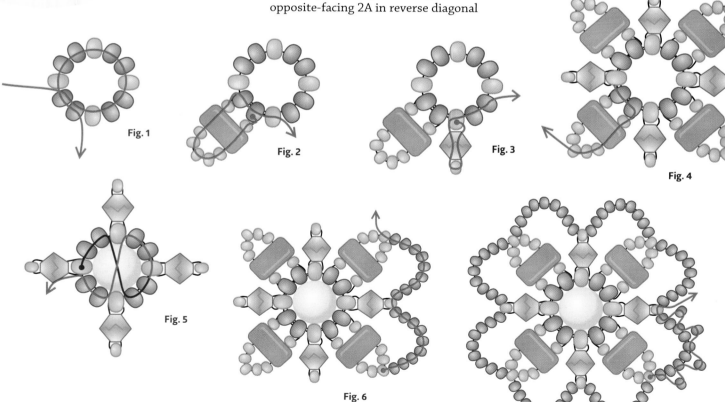

Fig. 1

Fig. 2

Fig. 3

Fig. 4

Fig. 5

Fig. 6

Fig. 7

9 Repeat Step 8 by weaving 1D into the third, fifth, seventh, and ninth Ds from Step 7 for the second arc. Pass through the third F (or center bead) of the picot above the brick (**Fig. 8**).

10 Repeat Steps 8–9 three times. Pass through the first D from Step 6 and the first D from Step 8.

11 String 2E and pass through the second D added in Step 8. Repeat adding 2E to the third and fourth Ds added in Step 8. Pass through the first D of the second arc (**Fig. 9**).

12 String 2E and pass through the second D added in Step 9. Repeat adding 2E to the third and fourth Ds added in Step 9. String 1D, 1B, and 1D. Pass through the first D of the third arc (**Fig. 10**).

13 Repeat Steps 11–12 three times. Set aside for assembly later.

14 Repeat Steps 1–13 five times to create a total of six components.

JOINING THE COMPONENTS

15 Lay the six components side by side. With Component 1, pass through the first 2E (to the left) of a bicone. String 1G and pass through the complementary opposite-facing 2E on Component 2. Pass through the last D of this arc into the first D of the next arc on Component 2. Continue to pass through the next 2E, the second hole of the G, and the opposite-facing 2E on Component 1. Pass through the last D of this arc into the first D and 2E of the next arc on Component 1 (**Fig. 11**).

16 Pass through the complementary opposite-facing 2E on Component 2 and through the opposite end of the 2E on Component 1 (**Fig. 12**).

Fig. 8

Fig. 9

Fig. 10

Fig. 11

Fig. 12

TIP
If you have loose tension, to stiffen the beadwork to reduce curling later, you can opt to reinforce the thread path from Steps 11–13 again.

17 Pass through the next D and the 2E of Component 1. String 1A. Continue to pass through the complementary opposite-facing 2E on Component 2, the opposite end of the 2E on Component 1, and the A added in this step **(Fig. 13)**.

18 To join the other end of Component 1 to Component 2, pass down the right side of Component 2 through 2E, 1D, 2E, 1D, 2E, and 1D of one arc, then down 1D, 2E, 1D, and 2E of the next arc. Flip the beadwork 180°.

19 Repeat Steps 16–17. Secure the thread and trim.

20 Repeat Steps 15–19 four times to connect the remaining components.

CREATING THE REVERSIBLE SNAP CLOSURE

21 With a 24" (61 cm) length of thread, string 2A, 1C, 2A, 1C, 2A, 1C, 2A, and 1C. Tie into a ring with a square knot, leaving a 12" (30.5 cm) tail. Pass through the first A.

22 String 1C, then pass through the next A and the following C on the ring. String 1E, 1 bicone, and 3F. Pass back through the bicone. String 1E and pass back through the C and the next A on the ring **(Fig. 14)**.

23 Repeat Step 22 three times around the ring. On the last step, pass through the first C added.

24 String 3F. Pass through the bicone. String 3F. Pass through the next C.

25 Repeat Step 24 three times **(Fig. 15)**.

26 Pass through all beads added from Steps 24–25 to align the beadwork. Set aside for assembly later.

27 Use the tail thread to add 1 pearl to the center. Pass through 2A. String 1 pearl and pass through the opposite-facing 2A in reverse diagonal direction

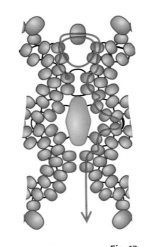

Fig. 13

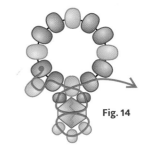

Fig. 14

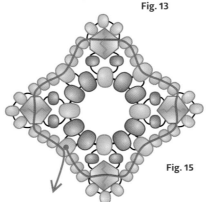

Fig. 15

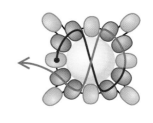

Fig. 16

Fig. 17

(Fig. 16, blue thread). Pass through 1B and 2A. Pass back through the pearl and the opposite-facing 2A in reverse diagonal direction **(Fig. 16, red thread)**. Flip the beadwork over to add the snap.

Note: The snap will be stitched where the ring of the 4C in Step 21 was created. Use the male portion of the snap with a flat back.

28 Pass through 1C, then string through one of the openings on the snap from the bottom up. Pass back through the C. Repeat this connection twice to secure the snap onto the beadwork. Pass through 2A and 1C.

29 Repeat Step 28 three times. Secure the tail thread and trim **(Fig. 17)**.

TIP

Make sure the snap side is facing up before stitching.

Fig. 18

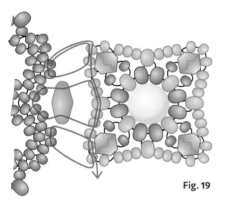

Fig. 19

30 Repeat Steps 21–26. *Note: The other side of the snap is made the same but without the pearl embellishment due to the domed back of the female side of the snap.*

31 Use the tail thread to pass through 2A and 1C. String 3D and pass through the C again **(Fig. 18, blue thread)**.

32 Repeat Step 31 three times. On the last repeat, pass back through the first 2D strung in the last repeat.

33 Pass through all second (or center) Ds added in Steps 31–32 to close the center of the beadwork to cover the snap. Reinforce by passing through the Ds twice **(Fig. 18, red thread)**.

34 Repeat Steps 28–29 to add the other side of the snap. Secure the tail thread and trim.

CONNECTING THE SNAP CLOSURE

35 Use the working thread from the snap with the pearl embellishment. Make sure the pearl side of the snap is facing up. Pass through the 3F added in Step 24 and the 3F added in Step 22 above the bicone. Pass through the second 2E on the top arc of Component 1.

Pass back through the second and third Fs on top of the bicone from the snap. Reinforce the connection **(Fig. 19)**.

36 Pass down through 3F, 1C, and 2F on the snap. String 1 brick. Pass through the first 2E on the bottom arc and the last 2E on the first arc of Component 1.

37 Pass through the second brick hole, the first 2F from Step 24, 1C, and the 2F on the snap. Reinforce the connection from Steps 36–37.

38 Pass through the last F from Step 24 and the first 2F from Step 22 on top of the third bicone embellishment of the snap. Pass through the second paired 2E on the bottom arc of Component 1. Pass back through the first and second Fs on top of the bicone from the snap. Reinforce the connection. Secure the thread and trim.

39 Repeat Steps 35–38 to connect the other side of the snap.

TECHNIQUES
Right-angle weave

Wrapped-loop bail

MATERIALS
0.7 g brown iris 11°
Japanese seed
beads (A)

0.2 g bronze 15°
Japanese seed
beads (B)

6 platinum 4mm
crystal pearls

2 valentinite
6.5×13mm crystal
drops

8 brown iris matte
6mm 2-hole triangles

2½" (6.5 cm) of gold-
filled 24-gauge wire

13" (33 cm) of gold-
filled 1.2mm cable
chain

1 pair of gold-filled
ear wires with
3mm ball

Smoke 6 lb braided
beading thread

TOOLS
Size 12 beading
needles

Round-nose pliers

Chain-nose pliers

Wire cutters

Ruler

Scissors

SIZE
2½" (6.5 cm)

LEVEL
Beginner

ISADORA

EARRINGS

Isadora Duncan was an American dancer during the Roaring Twenties. She was known for dancing with natural movements, emphasizing steps such as skipping. These earrings were inspired by the creator of Modern Contemporary Dance. The original design was reversed, but gravity and serendipity did their magic.

1 With a 60" (152.4 cm) length of thread, string 1 triangle and 2A. Pass through the second triangle hole. String 2A, then pass through the original triangle hole (**Fig. 1**).

2 Pass through the first 2A. String 1B, 2A, 1B, 2A, 1B, 2A, and 1B. Pass through the shared pair of As, then through the first six beads added in this step (**Fig. 2**).

3 String 1 triangle and 2A. Pass through the second triangle hole. Pass through the shared pair of As, then through the original triangle hole and the 2A added in this step. *Note: This step is similar to Step 1* (**Fig. 3**).

4 Repeat Step 2 but instead pass through the first three beads added in this step to create the "pointed" corner (**Fig. 4**).

5 Repeat Step 3 to add a new triangle and 2A (**Fig. 5**).

6 Rotate the beadwork to the left 90° or as desired for better visibility. Repeat Step 2 (**Fig. 6**).

7 Repeat Step 3 to add 1 triangle and 2A (**Fig. 7**).

8 Prepare and cut chain to six 1" (2.5 cm) lengths. *Note: There will be ½" (1.3 cm) of chain loss due to cutting.* For the cable chain, 1" (2.5 cm) of chain contains 24 links. String one chain. Follow the right-angle-weave thread path to reinforce the beadwork and add pearl embellishments. Pass through the adjacent paired As and string 1 pearl. Pass through the opposite-facing paired As in a diagonal direction. Circle around

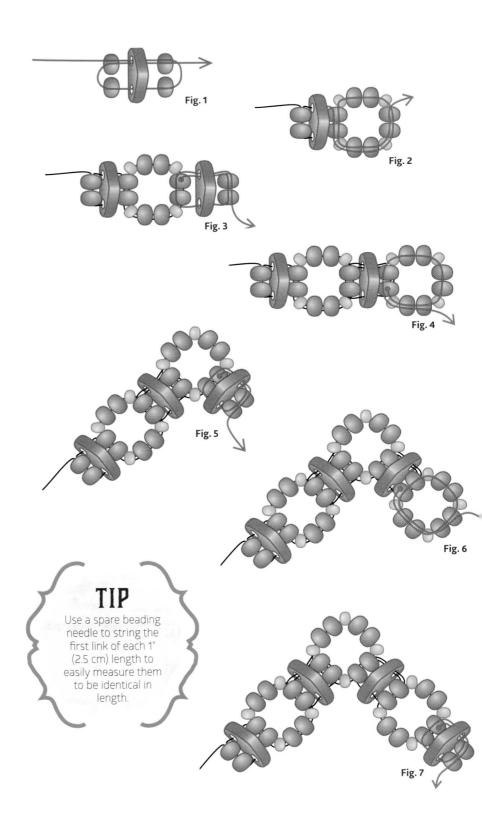

Fig. 1

Fig. 2

Fig. 3

Fig. 4

Fig. 5

Fig. 6

Fig. 7

TIP

Use a spare beading needle to string the first link of each 1" (2.5 cm) length to easily measure them to be identical in length.

Fig. 8

Fig. 9

through the beads following the right-angle-weave thread path of this unit until you reach the third B. String another chain and pass through the next 2A. String a third chain and pass through the B and the paired As adjacent to the triangle (**Fig. 8**).

9 Pass through the adjacent triangle again, following the right-angle-weave thread path, and then through the adjacent paired As. String 1 pearl and pass through the opposite-facing paired As in a diagonal direction. Circle around through the beads, following the right-angle-weave thread path of the top unit, until you reach the top corner B (**Fig. 9**).

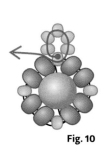

Fig. 10

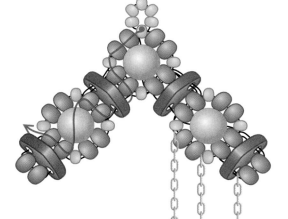

Fig. 11

Fig. 12

🔟 String 5B and pass through the original B of the top unit again. Reinforce the 5B two more times. *Note: This loop will be attached to the earring finding later* **(Fig. 10)**.

⓫ Pass through 2A, 1B, and the paired As adjacent to the triangle following the right-angle-weave thread path. Pass through the triangle and through the adjacent paired As on the opposite side. String 1 pearl. Pass through the opposite-facing paired As in a diagonal direction **(Fig. 11)**.

⓬ Circle around the beads, following the right-angle-weave thread path of this unit, until you reach the third B as in Step 8. String 1 chain and pass through the 2A. String 1 chain and pass through the B and the paired As adjacent to the final triangle. Pass through the triangle and the paired As on the opposite side. String the last chain. Follow the right-angle-weave thread path to secure the thread and trim. Use the tail thread to reinforce through the beadwork as in Step 8. Secure the tail thread and trim **(Fig. 12)**.

⓭ With 2½" (6.5 cm) of 24-gauge gold-filled wire, string the drop, leaving ⅜" (1 cm) of wire extended. Bend the wire with chain-nose pliers to follow the angle of the drop bead. Then bend both

wire ends ⅓" (8 mm) in line from the drop bead hole. Bend both wire ends to parallel and then trim the shorter wire end ¹⁄₁₂" (2 mm) past the bend. Create a ⅛" (3 mm) loop with the round-nose pliers. Before completing the wrapped loop, string all six chain ends in sequence, ensuring there is no twisting, and complete the wrapped loop with three or four wraps. As you wrap, capture the ¹⁄₁₂" (2 mm) wire length in the wraps. String the beaded loop created in Step 10 onto the earring hook through the front of the beadwork **(Fig. 13)**.

⓮ Repeat Steps 1–13 to create the second earring.

Fig. 13

← To create this variation, use lavender pearls, crystal lagoon drops, purple iris triangles, and blue gold luster seed beads for A.

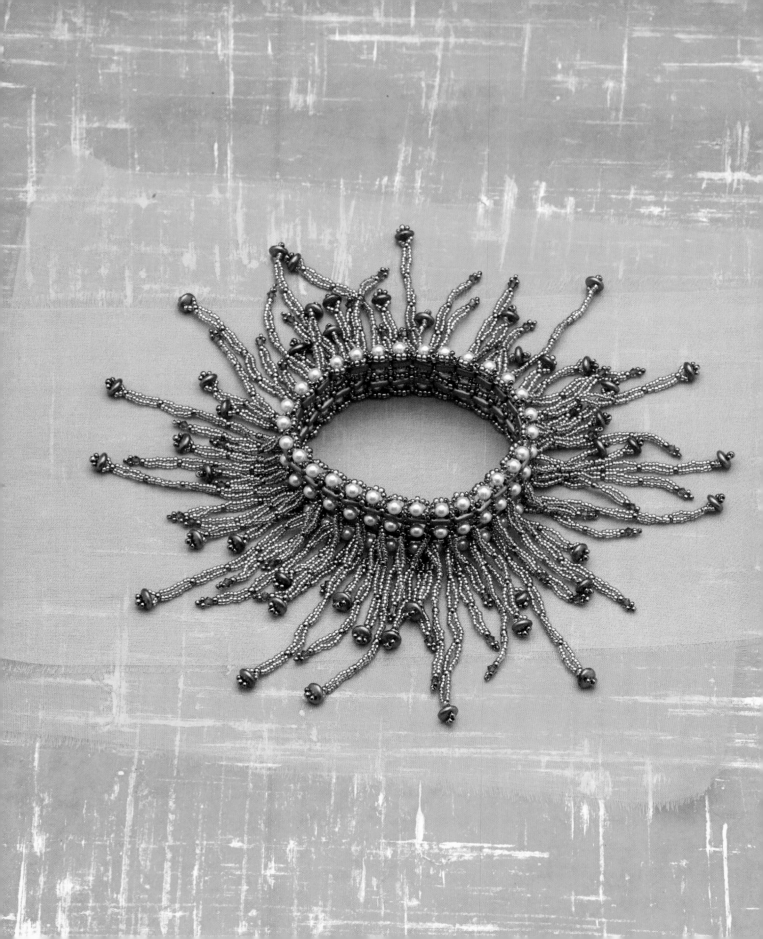

AUDREY FRINGE
BRACELET

Inspired by flapper-style dress embellishments, this right-angle-weave bangle incorporates three lengths of fringe on three tiers. This versatile design can be worn in two ways and easily modified to accommodate a clasp. The addition of pearl embellishments adds a classy, elegant, and timeless beauty to this bracelet named after my niece.

TECHNIQUES
Tubular right-angle weave

Fringe

MATERIALS
6 g bronze-lined aqua 11° Japanese seed beads (A)

4 g bronze 11° Japanese seed beads (B)

24 g bronze-lined aqua 15° Japanese seed beads (C)

3 g bronze 15° Japanese seed beads (D)

90 cream rose 4mm crystal pearls

45 blue zircon 3mm crystal bicones

60 gold matte 3×6mm Czech 2-hole bricks

45 gold matte 6mm Czech 2-hole lentils

Smoke 6 lb braided beading thread

TOOLS
Size 12 beading needles

No-Tangle bobbin or thread card

Bracelet gauge, tape measure, or ruler

Scissors

SIZE
7½" (19 cm)

LEVEL
Intermediate

TIPS

→ To measure the size of your bangle, make a fist (or place your thumb on top of your pinky) and use a bracelet gauge, tape measure, or piece of paper to measure the widest part of your hand. This is the inner bangle circumference measurement. The chart below helps you modify this pattern to fit your wrist. If you are between measurements, go up a size. Most people fall between a medium and a large bangle size; the instructions are for a medium-size bangle.

Bangle Size	Bangle Inner Diameter	Bangle Circumference	Estimated Number of Bricks to Use
XS	2.125 in. (5.6 cm)	6.67 in. (16.9cm)	26
S	2.25 in. (5.7 cm)	7.06 in. (17.9cm)	28
M	2.375 in. (6.0 cm)	7.45 in. (18.9cm)	30
L	2.5 in. (6.4 cm)	7.85 in. (19.9cm)	32
XL	2.625 in. (6.7 cm)	8.24 in. (20.0 cm)	34

→ The lack of a closure on this bracelet gives it a seamless look that easily slides on and off. If you prefer a bracelet with a clasp, select a five-strand slider tube clasp and create a base that has even counts of bricks so that the fringe balances out.

→ The bracelet can be worn in two ways, exposing or camouflaging the pearls.

1 With a 120" (304.8 cm) length of thread, wrap half of the length, or 60" (152.4 cm), on a thread card or No-Tangle bobbin. *Note: If you prefer using a shorter length, you can easily add more thread to the beadwork as you go.*

2 String 1 brick and 2A. Pass through the second hole of the brick on the same side. String 2A and pass back through to the original side of the remaining hole. Pass through the first 2A and the brick **(Fig. 1)**.

3 String 1A, 1 brick, and 1A. Pass through the adjoining hole of the first brick. Pass through the first A and the second brick **(Fig. 2)**.

4 Repeat Steps 2–3 twenty-nine times. On the last connection, join the thirtieth brick to the first brick to form a ring. This is Round 1 **(Fig. 3)**.

5 Pass through the first 2A on the first brick. String 1D, 2A, 1D, 2A, 1D, 2A, and 1D. Pass through the original 2A on the first brick and the first three beads strung **(Fig. 4)**.

Fig. 1

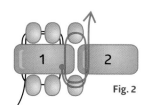

Fig. 2

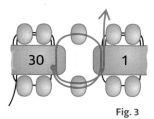

Fig. 3

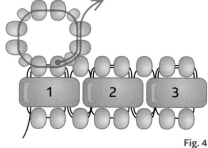

Fig. 4

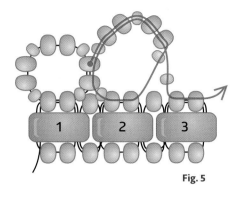

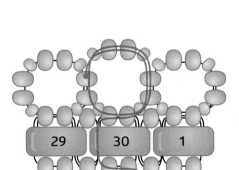

Fig. 5

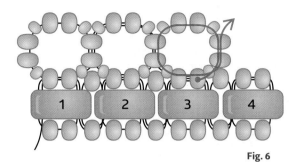

Fig. 6

Fig. 7

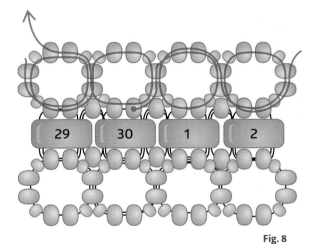

Fig. 8

6 String 1D, 2A, 1D, 2A, and 1D. Pass through the 2A on the second brick. String 1D and pass through the adjoining 2A from Step 5. Pass through all but the last D added in this step. String 1D and pass through the 2A on the third brick **(Fig. 5)**.

7 String 1D, 2A, 1D, 2A, and 1D. Pass through the adjoining 2A from Step 6. String 1D and pass through the 2A on the third brick and the first three beads strung in this step **(Fig. 6)**.

8 Repeat Steps 6–7 thirteen times.

9 For the last connection, string 1D, 2A, and 1D. Pass through the adjoining 2A from the first brick. String 1D and pass through the 2A on the thirtieth brick. String 1D and pass through the adjoining 2A, the first three beads strung, the adjoining 2A, 1D, and the 2A

on the thirtieth brick. Pass through the brick and the 2A on the other side of the thirtieth brick. This is Round 2 **(Fig. 7)**.

10 Flip the beadwork over. Repeat Steps 5–9 to create a second right-angle-weave round. This is Round 3.

11 *Note: Adding the second round of bricks is similar to the start, except one side of the brick will be joined to the respective 2A from the right-angle-weave round created in Step 10 (Round 3). To set up, after the connection from Step 10, pass through 1D and the adjoining 2A instead of through the brick. Then pass through 1D and 2A of the adjoining right-angle-weave link* **(Fig. 8)**.

TIP

The fringe accent beads can also be substituted with drops, Rizos, or mini daggers. Have fun mixing it up to create your own version.

12 String 1 brick and 2A. Pass through the second hole of the brick on the same side, the 2A on the right-angle-weave link below, the brick, the 2A strung in this step, and the brick. Repeat Step 3 **(Fig. 9)**.

13 Repeat Step 12 twenty-nine times to add a total of thirty bricks. On the last connection, join the thirtieth brick to the first brick to form a ring for this round. This is Round 4 **(Fig. 10)**.

14 Repeat Steps 5–9 to create a third right-angle-weave round. This is Round 5.

15 To set up for embellishing the right-angle-weave rounds (Rounds 2, 3, and 5), on the last connection from Step 14, pass through 1D and the adjoining 2A instead of through the brick.

16 String 1D, 1 pearl, and 1D. Pass through the opposite-facing 2A in reverse diagonal direction **(Fig. 11)**.

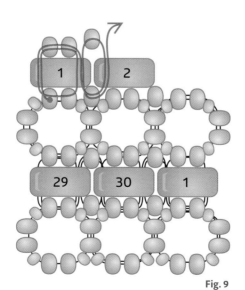

Fig. 9

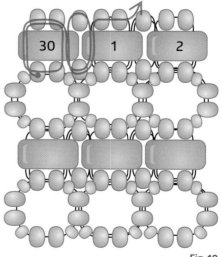

Fig. 10

17 Repeat Step 16 twenty-nine times. This embellishes Round 5. Secure the thread and trim.

18 Add a new thread to embellish the center right-angle-weave round (Round 3). Use about 15" (38 cm) or a comfortable length of thread. Repeat Steps 16–17. This embellishes Round 3. Secure both ends of thread and trim.

19 Unwind the remaining thread from the thread card to embellish the last (Round 2) right-angle-weave round and create the fringes. Repeat Steps 16–17.

20 After adding the last pearl embellishment from Step 19, pass counterclockwise through 1D, 2A, 1D, 2A, 1D, 2A, 1D, 2A, and 1D of the last right-angle-weave link.

21 String 1B, 9C, 1B, 9C, 1B, 9C, 1B, 1 bicone, and 3D. Pass through the bicone and fourth B. String 9C and pass through the third B. Repeat twice, stringing 9C through the second and first Bs. Pass clockwise (to the right) through 1D, 2A, and the D of the next link.

22 String 1B, 9C, 1B, 9C, 1B, 2C, 1 lentil, and 3D. Pass through the second hole of the lentil. String 2C and pass through the third B. String 9C and pass through the second B. Repeat, stringing 9C through the first B. Pass clockwise (to the right) through 1D, 2A, and 1D of the next link **(Fig. 12)**.

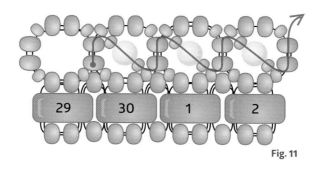

| 29 | 30 | 1 | 2 |

Fig. 11

Fig. 12

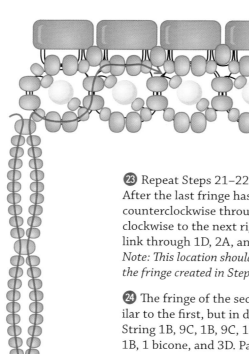
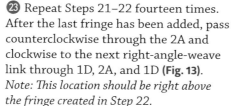

Fig. 13

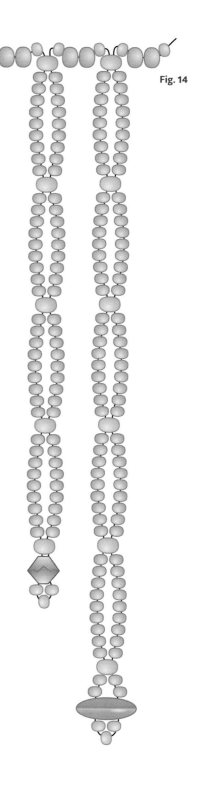

Fig. 14

23 Repeat Steps 21–22 fourteen times. After the last fringe has been added, pass counterclockwise through the 2A and clockwise to the next right-angle-weave link through 1D, 2A, and 1D **(Fig. 13)**. *Note: This location should be right above the fringe created in Step 22.*

24 The fringe of the second level is similar to the first, but in different lengths. String 1B, 9C, 1B, 9C, 1B, 9C, 1B, 9C, 1B, 1 bicone, and 3D. Pass through the bicone and the fifth B. String 9C and pass through the fourth B. Repeat three times, stringing 9C through the third, the second, and the first Bs. Pass clockwise (to the right) through 1D, 2A, and 1D of the next link.

25 String 1B, 9C, 1B, 9C, 1B, 9C, 1B, 9C, 1B, 9C, 1B, 2C, 1 lentil, and 3D. Pass through the second hole of the lentil. String 2C and pass through the sixth B. String 9C and pass through the fifth B. Repeat four times, stringing 9C through the fourth, the third, the second, and the first Bs. Pass clockwise (to the right) through the D, 2A, and the D of the next link **(Fig. 14)**.

26 Repeat Steps 24–25 fourteen times. After the last fringe has been added, pass through 1D, 2A, and the brick and counterclockwise through the 2A and 1D on the opposite side of brick in the next link. *Note: This location should be right above the fringe created in Step 24. To add the fringe on the last tier, the beading direction will now move left. The fringes on this level are created the same as in Steps*

21–22 but with the bottom embellishments switched between the bicones and lentils.

27 String 1B, 9C, 1B, 9C, 1B, 1 bicone, and 3D. Pass through the bicone and third B. String 9C and pass through the second B. Repeat, stringing 9C through the first B. Pass counterclockwise (to the left) through 1D, 2A, and 1D of the next link **(Fig. 15)**.

28 String 1B, 9C, 1B, 9C, 1B, 9C, 1B, 2C, a lentil, and 3D. Pass through the second hole of the lentil. String 2C and pass through the fourth B. String 9C and pass through the third B. Repeat twice, string-ing 9C through the second and the first Bs. Pass counterclockwise (to the left) through 1D, 2A, and 1D of the next link.

29 Repeat Steps 27–28 fourteen times. After the last fringe has been added, secure the thread following the right-angle-weave-thread path and trim.

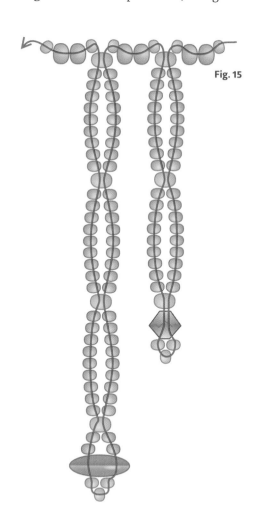

Fig. 15

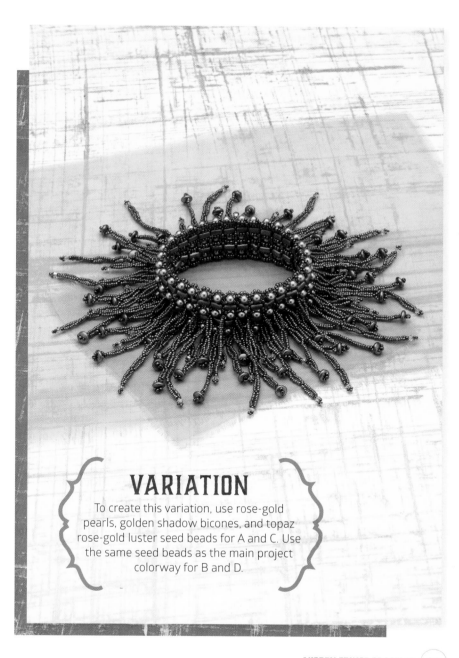

VARIATION

To create this variation, use rose-gold pearls, golden shadow bicones, and topaz rose-gold luster seed beads for A and C. Use the same seed beads as the main project colorway for B and D.

RIVOLI SCALLOP CHAIN
EARRINGS

═══════════

I often use fine chain in my earring designs because it adds a sense of fluidity with the tiniest bit of movement. The scalloped three-tiered chains are sewn onto the rivoli bezel. The cascading effect is reminiscent of the hemlines of flapper-style dresses of the Roaring Twenties.

TECHNIQUES
Circular peyote stitch

Stitch-in-the-ditch embellishment

Picot

MATERIALS
1.5 g topaz rose-gold luster 11° Japanese seed beads (A)

1 g bronze 11° Japanese seed beads (B)

0.5 g topaz rose-gold luster 15° Japanese seed beads (C)

1 g bronze 15° Japanese seed beads (D)

2 heliotrope 14mm rhinestone rivolis

37" (94 cm) of gold-filled 2.25mm flat cable chain

1 pair of gold-filled lever-back ear wires

Smoke 6 lb braided beading thread

TOOLS
Size 12 beading needles

Wire cutters

Ruler

Scissors

SIZE
3" (7.5 cm)

LEVEL
Beginner

41

1 With 36" (91.5 cm) of thread, string 32A and join into a ring with a square knot, leaving an 8" (20.5 cm) tail. Pass through 1A away from the knot.

2 **ROUNDS 1–3:** Begin circular peyote stitch. String 1A, skip 1A on the ring, and pass through the next A. Repeat fifteen times. Step up through the first A added in this round.

ROUND 4: Work circular peyote stitch with 1A. Step up through the first A added in this round.

ROUND 5: Work circular peyote stitch with 1C. Step up through the first C added in this round.

ROUND 6: Work circular peyote stitch with 1D. Step up through the first D added in this round (**Fig. 1**).

3 Insert the rivoli facedown into the bezel just created. The first round of peyote will then be facing up (**Fig. 2**).

4 **ROUND 7:** Using the tail thread, work circular peyote stitch with 1C into the As from Round 1. Step up through the first C added in this round.

ROUND 8: Work circular peyote stitch with 1D. Step up through the first D added in this round. Secure the tail thread and trim.

5 Prepare and cut chain for the scallops. *Note: There will be about 1" (2.5 cm) of chain lost due to cutting.* Cut a length of each of the following: 1" (2.5 cm), 1½" (3.8 cm), 2" (5 cm), 2½" (6.4 cm), 3" (7.5 cm), 3½" (9 cm), and 4" (10 cm). Separate the chains by size and arrange in this order on the work surface.

6 Flip the beadwork to the front. Pass through 1A on Round 4 and stitch-in-the-ditch with 1B, passing through each A on Round 4. Step up through the first B added in this round (**Fig. 3**).

7 String 3D and pass through the next B added in Step 6. Repeat fifteen times to create a picot edging (**Fig. 4**).

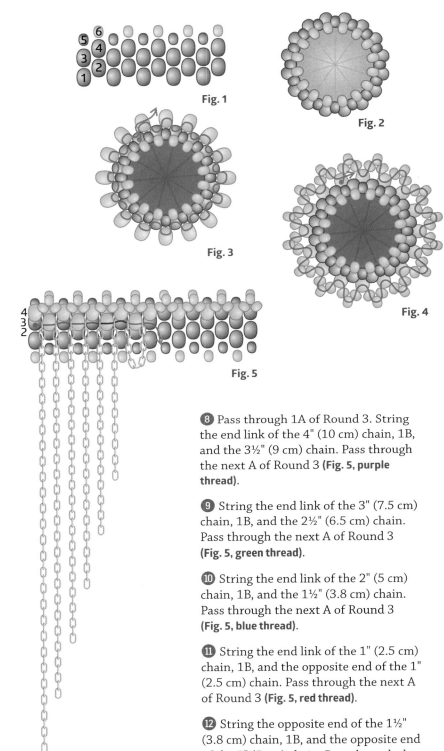

Fig. 1

Fig. 2

Fig. 3

Fig. 4

Fig. 5

8 Pass through 1A of Round 3. String the end link of the 4" (10 cm) chain, 1B, and the 3½" (9 cm) chain. Pass through the next A of Round 3 (**Fig. 5, purple thread**).

9 String the end link of the 3" (7.5 cm) chain, 1B, and the 2½" (6.5 cm) chain. Pass through the next A of Round 3 (**Fig. 5, green thread**).

10 String the end link of the 2" (5 cm) chain, 1B, and the 1½" (3.8 cm) chain. Pass through the next A of Round 3 (**Fig. 5, blue thread**).

11 String the end link of the 1" (2.5 cm) chain, 1B, and the opposite end of the 1" (2.5 cm) chain. Pass through the next A of Round 3 (**Fig. 5, red thread**).

12 String the opposite end of the 1½" (3.8 cm) chain, 1B, and the opposite end of the 2" (5 cm) chain. Pass through the next A of Round 3.

13 String the opposite end of the 2½" (6.5 cm) chain, 1B, and the opposite end

Fig. 6

of the 3" (7.5 cm) chain. Pass through the next A of Round 3.

14 String the opposite end of the 3½" (9 cm) chain, 1B, and the opposite end of the 4" (10 cm) chain. Pass through the next A of Round 3.

15 String 1B and pass through an A of Round 3 four times.

16 String 1B, 2D, the lever-back ear wire, and 2D. Pass through the B again to create a loop. Reinforce this connection loop, then pass through the next A of Round 3 (**Fig. 6, blue thread**).

17 Continue to string 1B and pass through 1A of Round 3 four times (**Fig. 6, red thread**).

18 Pass through all the Bs and chain added from Steps 8–17 to reinforce the connections. Secure the thread and trim.

19 Repeat Steps 1–18 for the second earring.

↓ To create this variation, use aqua rivolis and metallic nebula seed beads for A and C, dark silver seed beads for B and D, sterling silver flat cable chain, and sterling silver leverback ear wires.

{VARIATIONS}

↓ To create this variation, use light vitrail rivolis and purple-lined rainbow rosaline seed beads for A and C. Use the same seed beads as the main project colorway for B and D.

← To create this variation, use crystal rivolis, periwinkle gray luster seed beads for A and C, dark silver seed beads for B and D, sterling silver flat cable chain, and sterling silver leverback ear wires.

CHRYSANTHEMUM
BROOCH

───────────────

I can't escape Mother Nature's influence in my beadwork. This brooch design was actually first inspired by the Rizo rice drop bead. Daggers are available in many sizes and are often used for floral designs. The Rizos were the perfect shape to evoke a chrysanthemum and gave the dimensional appearance I desired. This design also explores bezeling a circle pin back.

TECHNIQUES

Circular peyote stitch

Ladder stitch

Stitch-in-the-ditch embellishment

Picot

MATERIALS

2.5 g topaz rose-gold luster 11° Japanese seed beads (A)

1 g bronze 11° Japanese seed beads (B)

0.5 g topaz rose-gold luster 15° Japanese seed beads (C)

1 g bronze 15° Japanese seed beads (D)

1 volcano 16mm rivoli rhinestone

18 magic copper 2.5×6mm pressed-glass rice drops

18 copper iris 3×11mm daggers

1 steel 16mm circular pin back

Double-sided 1" (2.5 cm) tape

Smoke 6 lb braided beading thread

TOOLS

Size 12 beading needles

Scissors

SIZE

1½" (3.8 cm)

LEVEL

Intermediate

TIPS

→ If you prefer a pendant instead of a pin, you can easily add a peyote bail loop to the design through the third peyote row in lieu of adding the pin back. You can also use a number of different brooch-to-pendant converters available in the market.

→ The chrysanthemum makes a great focal piece for a bracelet. Add a bracelet band to the focal through the third peyote row.

→ If you like to wear floral rings, a peyote or right-angle-weave band can be easily implemented.

→ To change up the look and create a different flower, use long drops and different sizes of daggers.

① With a 60" (152.4 cm) length of thread, string 36A and join into a ring with a square knot, leaving an 8" (20.5 cm) tail. Pass through 1A away from the knot.

② **ROUNDS 1–3:** Begin circular peyote stitch. String 1A, skip 1A on the ring, and pass through the next A. Repeat seventeen times. Step up through the first A added in this round **(Fig. 1, orange thread)**.

③ **ROUNDS 4–5:** Work circular peyote stitch with 1A. Step up through the first A added in the respective round **(Fig. 1, green thread)**.

④ **ROUNDS 6–7:** Work circular peyote stitch with 1C. Step up through the first C added in the respective round **(Fig. 1, blue thread)**.

⑤ **ROUND 8:** Work circular peyote stitch with 1D. Step up through the first D added in this round **(Fig. 1, red thread)**.

⑥ Insert the rivoli facedown into the bezel just created. The first round of peyote stitch will then be facing up **(Fig. 2)**.

⑦ **ROUND 9:** Using the tail thread, work circular peyote stitch with C into the A from Round 1. Step up through the first C added in this round.

⑧ **ROUND 10:** Work circular peyote stitch with C. Step up through the first C added in this round.

⑨ **ROUND 11:** Work circular peyote stitch with D. Step up through the first D added in this round. Secure the thread and trim.

⑩ Flip the beadwork to the front. Pass through 1A on Round 5 and stitch-in-the-ditch with a B passing through each A from Round 5. Step up through the first B added in this round **(Fig. 3)**.

⑪ String 3D and pass through the next B added in Step 10. Repeat seventeen more times to create a picot edging **(Fig. 4)**.

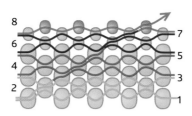

Fig. 1

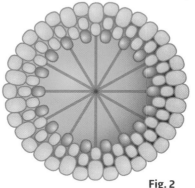

Fig. 2

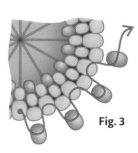

Fig. 3

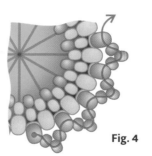

Fig. 4

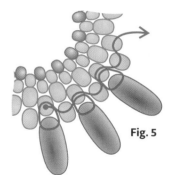

Fig. 5

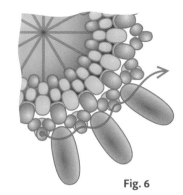

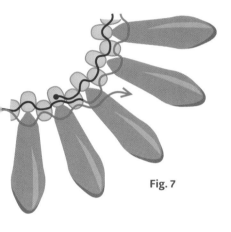

Fig. 6

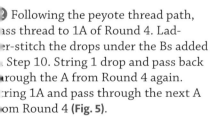

Fig. 7

Following the peyote thread path, pass thread to 1A of Round 4. Ladder-stitch the drops under the Bs added in Step 10. String 1 drop and pass back through the A from Round 4 again. String 1A and pass through the next A from Round 4 **(Fig. 5)**.

Repeat Step 12 seventeen times. Step up through the first drop added. There should be a total of eighteen drops and 18A added.

Note: The drops need to be aligned properly through the center bead of the picots added in Step 11. Pass through the second (or center bead) of the picot from Step 11, then through the next drop. To stiffen and align the drops, pass through the thread path again **(Fig. 6)**.

15 Following the peyote-stitch thread path, pass thread to 1A of Round 3. String 1A and pass through the next A of Round 3. Repeat seventeen times, adding 1A to each of the As of Round 3. Step up through the first A added in this step **(Fig. 7, blue thread)**.

16 String 1 dagger and pass through the next A added in Step 15. Repeat seventeen times, adding 1 dagger to each of the As from Step 15. Step up on the last stitch by passing through the first dagger added. To stiffen and align the daggers, pass through the thread path again **(Fig. 7, red thread)**.

17 Following the peyote-stitch thread path, pass through 1A of Round 1. String 1A and pass through the next 1A from Round 1. Repeat seventeen times, adding 1A to each of the As from Round 1. Step up through the first A added in this step.

18 Apply the double-sided tape to the back of the pin-back finding. Trim around the edge. *Note: The double-sided tape helps the pin-back finding stay in place while securing it to the back of the beadwork.* Adhere the finding to the back of the beadwork, taking care to ensure the pin connections are between two As from Step 17 **(Fig. 8)**.

19 String 3A and pass through 1A from Step 17. Repeat seventeen times, adding 3A to each of the As from Step 17. Step up through the first 2As added in this step. This is the second (or center) bead **(Fig. 9, green thread)**.

20 String 3A and pass through the center A of the next picot added in Step 19. Repeat, adding 3A to each of the center As from Step 19. Step up through the first 2As added in this step **(Fig. 9, blue thread)**.

21 String 2D and pass through the next center A added in Step 20. Repeat, adding 2D to each of the center As from Step 20. Step up through the first 2Ds added in this step **(Fig. 9, red thread)**.

22 Pass through all beads added in Step 21 again to tighten the beadwork. Secure the thread and trim.

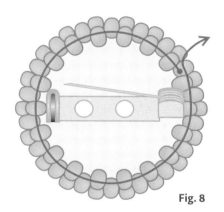

Fig. 8

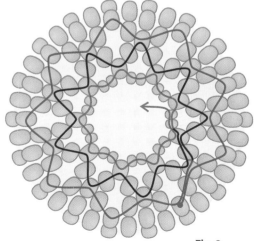

Fig. 9

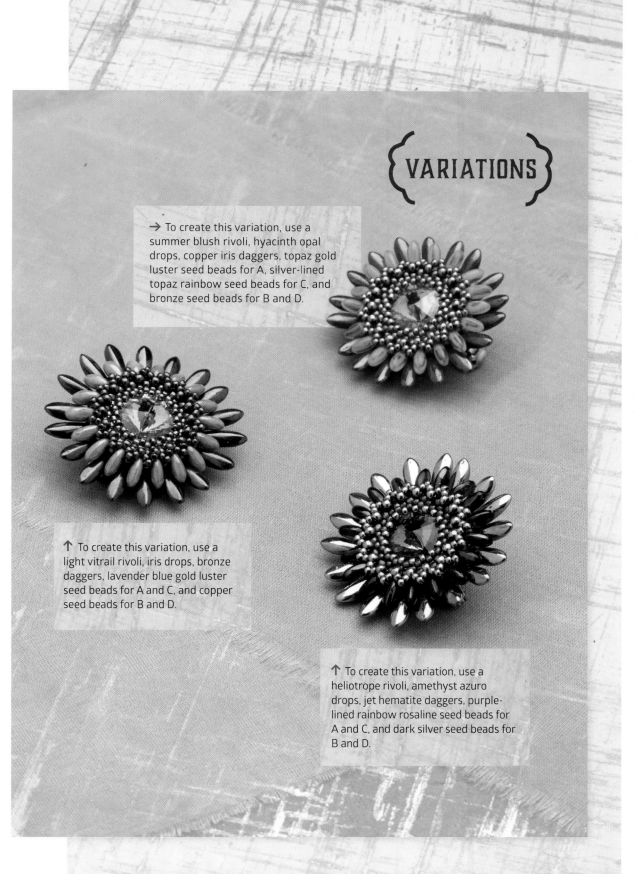

{ VARIATIONS }

→ To create this variation, use a summer blush rivoli, hyacinth opal drops, copper iris daggers, topaz gold luster seed beads for A, silver-lined topaz rainbow seed beads for C, and bronze seed beads for B and D.

↑ To create this variation, use a light vitrail rivoli, iris drops, bronze daggers, lavender blue gold luster seed beads for A and C, and copper seed beads for B and D.

↑ To create this variation, use a heliotrope rivoli, amethyst azuro drops, jet hematite daggers, purple-lined rainbow rosaline seed beads for A and C, and dark silver seed beads for B and D.

TECHNIQUES
Peyote stitch

Circular peyote stitch

Tubular peyote stitch

Stitch-in-the-ditch embellishment

Netting

Cubic right-angle weave

Square stitch

Picot

MATERIALS
25 g dark topaz gold luster 11° Japanese seed beads (A)

1 g bronze 11° Japanese seed beads (B)

1 g dark topaz gold luster 15° Japanese seed beads (C)

2 g bronze 15° Japanese seed beads (D)

2 volcano 12mm rivoli rhinestones

1 astral pink 30×20mm rhinestone drop

45 cream 2mm Czech glass pearls

16 mauve 3mm fire-polished glass rounds

1 black 3/0 sew-on snap set

Smoke 6 lb braided beading thread

TOOLS
Size 12 beading needles

No-Tangle bobbin

Scissors

SIZE
19.5" (49.5 cm)

LEVEL
Advanced

SUNDARA
NECKLACE

Inspired by Maharaja Indian jewelry with a mix of romantic flair, Sundara is Hindu for "beautiful." During the 1800s, the European royal courts and upper middle class were crazy over seed pearl designs. Jewelers imported the pearls from India and China. Many designs of the time were encrusted with seed pearls accenting gemstones. Cubic right-angle weave is the predominant stitch used in both the necklace and the pearl pendant bezel.

CREATING THE PENDANT BEZEL

1 With a 120" (304.8 cm) length of thread, wrap half onto a No-Tangle bobbin. *Note: A cubic right-angle-weave bezel is created for the crystal drop. Think of a cube with six walls as you create each cubic right-angle-weave (CRAW) unit. Two units have a common wall.* String 4A. Pass through the first 2A strung again. You've created the first wall **(Fig. 1)**.

2 String 3A. Pass through the original A from the first wall and the first 2A added in this step. You've created the second wall **(Fig. 2)**.

3 String 3A. Pass through the adjoining A from the second wall and the first 2A added in this step. You've created the third wall and three units of flat right-angle weave **(Fig. 3)**.

4 To create the cube shape, the third wall is joined to the first wall to create the fourth wall. String 1A. Pass through the complementary unattached A of the first wall. String 1A. Pass through the original A of the third wall. This creates the fourth wall. Pass through the first A added in this step **(Fig. 4)**.

5 To create the fifth wall, the top 4A are unattached. Pass through the other 3A and the original A to close the fifth wall **(Fig. 5)**.

6 Make a right-angle turn and pass through the side A. Repeat with another right-angle turn and pass through the bottom A **(Fig. 6)**.

7 Flip the beadwork over so the bottom is now the top with the thread orientation as in Step 5. Repeat Step 5 to secure the beads to close the sixth and final wall. This is the first CRAW unit **(Fig. 7)**.

8 *Note: The last wall (sixth wall in the first CRAW unit) is now the first wall of the second CRAW unit. There is always a shared wall between the CRAW unit you just completed and the next CRAW unit you are to start.* String 3A. Pass through the original A and the A of the first wall (common wall). The second wall of this unit has been created **(Fig. 8)**.

9 String 2A. Pass through the side A of the second wall, the original A, and the next A of the first wall. The third wall has been created **(Fig. 9)**.

10 Rotate the beadwork 90° to the right for better visibility as you bead the walls. String 2A. Pass through the side A of the third wall, the original A, the last A of the first wall, and up through the side A of the second wall. The fourth wall has been created **(Fig. 10)**.

11 The fifth wall is only missing its top A. String 1A. Pass down the side A of the fourth wall, the side A of the first wall, the side A of the second wall, and the A added in this step. The fifth wall has been created **(Fig. 11)**.

12 *Note: Closing the sixth wall creates a firmer rope. I find it easier to see the common wall as you proceed to increase the CRAW rope length.* Pass through all top As and the original A from the fifth wall. The sixth wall has been created. Repeat Steps 8–12, being mindful of the weaving direction. Each CRAW unit will alternate in beading direction, switching from clockwise to counterclockwise. Build a rope with a total of 28 CRAW units **(Fig. 12)**.

13 Join the twenty-eighth CRAW unit to the side wall of the first CRAW unit at 90° to create a point. Two walls have already been created. String 1A. Pass through the side A of the first CRAW unit. String 1A. Pass through the original A of the twenty-eighth CRAW unit and the first A added in this step. The third wall has been created **(Fig. 13)**.

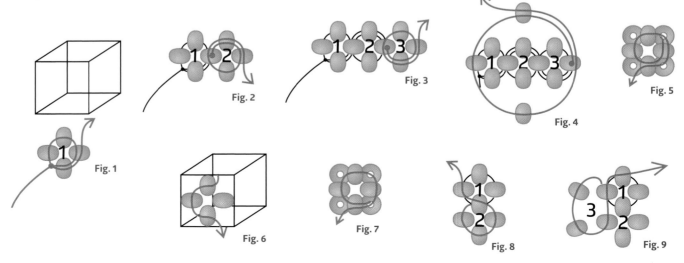

Fig. 1
Fig. 2
Fig. 3
Fig. 4
Fig. 5
Fig. 6
Fig. 7
Fig. 8
Fig. 9

14 The next wall is only missing its top A. Pass through the side A from the first CRAW unit. String 1A. Pass through the side A of the twenty-eighth CRAW unit, the A added in Step 13, and the side A from the first CRAW unit. This creates the fourth wall (**Fig. 14**).

15 Rotate the beadwork 90° for beading visibility. Pass through the side A of the first CRAW unit. Repeat Step 14 to create the fifth wall. Repeat Step 5 to connect all As to close up the sixth wall. Circle around twice to secure the join (**Fig. 15**). *Note: This wall is inside the bezel. A drop bezel edge has been created, but in order to secure the crystal drop in place, more beadwork is added to the front and back inside edges to capture the drop securely.*

16 Pass through to the A of the twenty-ninth CRAW unit to the inside edge of the bezel. Use circular peyote stitch to add a bezel lip to both the front and the back of the bezel to lock the drop in place. Pass through to the A of the second CRAW unit to join at the base of the point. String 1B. Pass through the next A of the subsequent CRAW unit. Repeat twenty-six times. Step up to the first B added in this step (**Fig. 16**).

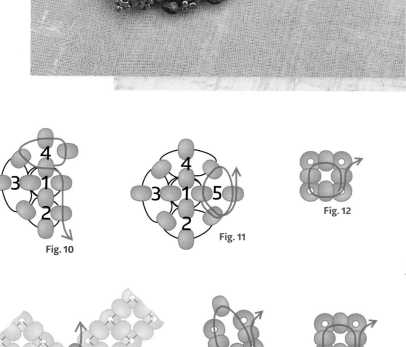

Fig. 10

Fig. 11

Fig. 12

Fig. 13

Fig. 14

Fig. 15

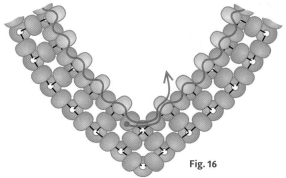

Fig. 16

17 String 1D, then pass through the next B. Repeat twenty-six times but do not step up yet **(Fig. 17)**.

18 String 1D between the last and first Bs from Step 16 to close up the bezel point. Step up through the first D added in Step 17 **(Fig. 18)**.

19 String 3D, then pass through the next D added in Step 17, the B, and the following D. Repeat twelve times **(Fig. 19)**.

20 Step up by passing through the first B added in Step 16, the D from Step 17, and through all 3D of the first 3-bead picot added in Step 19 **(Fig. 20)**.

21 String 1B, then pass through all 3D of the next 3-bead picot **(Fig. 21)**. Repeat around twelve times. On the last repeat, pass through the first 3-bead picot. Secure the thread and trim. Unwind the tail thread from the No-Tangle bobbin. Pass through to the same location as in Step 16 but to the front side of the bezel's inside edge.

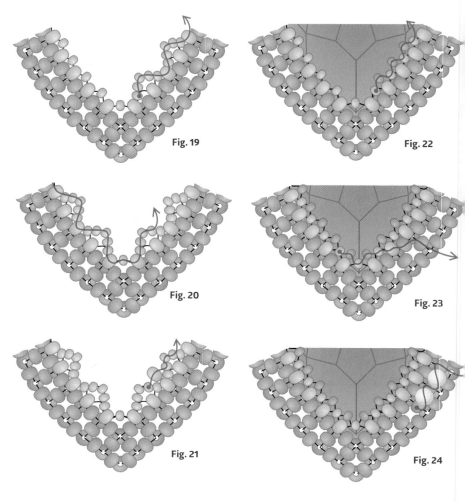

Fig. 19

Fig. 20

Fig. 21

Fig. 22

Fig. 23

Fig. 24

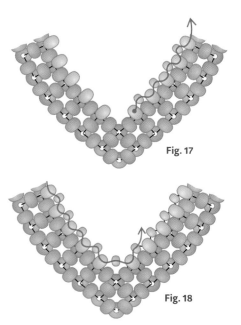

Fig. 17

Fig. 18

22 Place the crystal drop into the bezel faceup. Next, surface beadwork will be added as in the back to secure the rhinestone fully in place. Repeat Steps 16–18 as in the back bezel. String 1C, then pass through the next D added in the previous step. Repeat twenty-six times **(Fig. 22)**.

23 Following the right-angle-weave thread path, pass through the side A of the CRAW unit three away to the right of the bezel point **(Fig. 23)**.

24 String a pearl. Pass through the opposite-facing A in a diagonal direction. Repeat around twenty-five more times **(Fig. 24)**.

25 To turn at the bezel point, pass through the remaining As of this CRAW unit **(Fig. 25)**. Repeat Step 24 three more times to complete the pearl embellishments. There should be twenty-nine pearls added in total.

26 Pass through the first pearl embellishment and its side edge A **(Fig. 26)**. Rotate the beadwork to embellish the bezel's side edge.

27 String 1A, then pass through the A on the outer bezel edge. String 3D, then pass through the next A on the outer bezel edge. Repeat this entire step once more. **(Fig. 27)**.

28 At the bezel point there are three 3-bead picots of Ds for accenting. One set was added in Step 27. String 3D, then pass through the next A on the outer bezel edge. Repeat once more. Repeat Step 27 thirteen times. Pass through the first A added from Step 27, the adjoining A on the outer bezel edge, and the first D from the 3-bead picot **(Fig. 28)**.

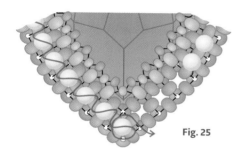

Fig. 25

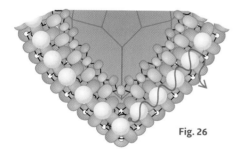

Fig. 26

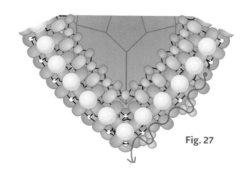

Fig. 27

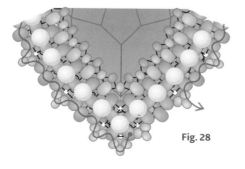

Fig. 28

29 String 1C, then pass through the first D and the next D again. Repeat with another C, creating two square stitches. String 1 fire-polished round, then pass through the next A added in Step 27 and the adjoining A on the outer bezel edge. At the bezel point, to stiffen the beadwork, pass through all three 3-bead picots and their adjoining As on the outer bezel edge (**Fig. 29**).

30 The opposite left side of the pendant embellishment is a mirror image to the right side just completed. Repeat Step 29 but in reverse order. String 1 fire-

polished round, then pass through the second D of the picot. String 1C, then pass through the second and the last D of the picot. String 1C, then pass back through the last D of the picot, the adjoining A on the outer bezel edge, and the subsequent A added in Step 27. Repeat this entire step five times. You are now at the opposite-facing center to the bezel point (**Fig. 30**).

31 String 1 fire-polished round, then pass through the second D of the subsequent 3-bead picot. String 3D, then pass through the second D of the picot again. String 1 fire-polished round, then pass through the A added in Step 27, the adjoining A on the outer bezel edge, and the first D of the subsequent 3-bead picot (**Fig. 31**). Repeat Step 29 five times.

32 The square-stitched embellishments need to be aligned and the beadwork stiffened. Pass through the two C square stitches. String 1C, then pass through

the fire-polished round and the A added in Step 27. At the bezel point, pass through all three 3-bead picots and their adjoining As from the outer bezel edge. After the last picot, pass through the subsequent A from Step 27 (**Fig. 32**).

33 Pass through the fire-polished round. String 1C, then pass through the two C square stitches and the A added in Step 27. Repeat five times (**Fig. 33**).

34 At the midpoint of the bezel, pass through the fire-polished round, the 3C, the fire-polished round, and the A from Step 27. Repeat Step 32 five times (**Fig. 34**).

35 Pass thread to the back following the right-angle-weave thread path along the side walls of the CRAW edge until reaching the A on the outer edge beads directly behind the midpoint of the bezel. This location is at the back of the 3-bead picot between the two fire-polished round beads. Set aside for assembly later (**Fig. 35**).

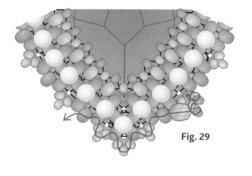

Fig. 29

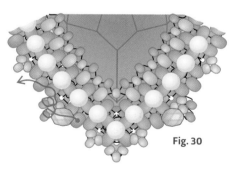

Fig. 30

Fig. 31

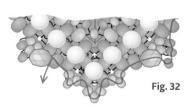

Fig. 32

Fig. 33

Fig. 34

Fig. 35

ADDING THE RIVOLI BAIL ACCENT

36 With a 60" (152.4 cm) length of thread, string 28A and join into a ring with a square knot, leaving an 8" (20.5 cm) tail. Pass through 1A away from the knot.

37 ROUNDS 1–3: Begin circular peyote stitch. String 1A, skip 1A from the ring, and pass through the next A. Repeat around fourteen times. Step up through the first A added in this round.

ROUND 4: Work circular peyote stitch with 1A. Step up through the first A added in this round.

ROUND 5: Work circular peyote stitch with 1C. Step up through the first C added in this round.

ROUND 6: Work circular peyote stitch with 1D. Step up through the first D added in this round **(Fig. 36)**.

38 Insert the rivoli facedown into the bezel just created. The first round of peyote will then be facing up.

39 ROUND 7: Using the tail thread, work circular peyote stitch with 1C into the A from Round 1. Step up through the first C added in this round.

ROUND 8: Work circular peyote stitch with 1D. Step up through the first D added in this round. Secure the tail thread and trim. Flip the beadwork over to the front **(Fig. 37)**.

40 Pass through 1A on Round 4 and stitch-in-the-ditch with a B passing through each A on Round 4 **(Fig. 38)**. Step up through the first B added in this step.

41 String 3D, then pass through the next B added in Step 40 **(Fig. 39)**. Repeat thirteen more times to create a picot edging. Step up through the second D of the first picot added in this step.

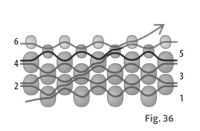

Fig. 36

Fig. 37

Fig. 38

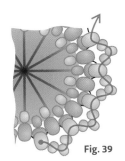

Fig. 39

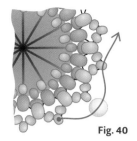

Fig. 40

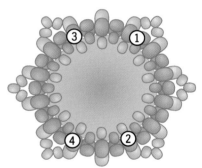

Bail Guides   **Fig. 41**

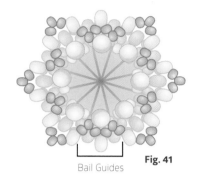

③ ①
④ ②

Fig. 42

42 The ornate border is created by stitching some of the center D picot beads together with 2mm pearls, while leaving others unattached to create points. String 1 pearl, skip a picot, and pass through the next center picot bead **(Fig. 40)**. Repeat twice.

43 String 1 pearl. Pass through the next center D picot bead. Repeat Step 42 three times. Repeat this step again. Circle around the connected picots and pearls to tighten around the bezel.

44 To create the bail loop, pass through to the A in Round 1 directly aligned with the D noted as bail guides in **Fig. 41**. *Note: The connections are at Locations 1, 2, 3, and 4 on* **Fig. 42**.

45 From Location 1, string 13A. Pass through the opposite-facing A on the bezel bottom, Location 2. Pass back through the beads strung and into the opposite end of the original A on the bezel top, Location 1. Following the pey-ote-stitched thread path, pass through the A in Round 2, the A in Round 1, then back to the next A in Round 2 to Location 3 **(Fig. 43)**.

46 Repeat Step 45 and string 13A. Pass through the opposite-facing A on the bezel bottom, Location 4. Pass back through the beads strung and into the opposite end of the original A on the bezel top, Location 3 **(Fig. 44)**.

47 Pass down through the first 4A from Step 46. A reverse square stitch is added to join the A strands added in Steps 45–46 to create a sturdier bail loop. Pass back up the complementary fourth A from Step 45, then back down the original A and the fifth A from Step 46. Repeat six times. Pass down through the remaining 3A from Step 46 to Location 4. Set aside the rivoli bail accent for assembly later **(Fig. 45)**.

FORMING THE CRAW ROPE

48 As in the CRAW bezel, repeat Steps 1–12 until an 18" (45.5 cm) CRAW rope is created. *Note: The rope I created had 13 CRAW units. To create a longer rope, there are about eight CRAW units to 1" (2.5 cm).* With a 120" (308.4 cm) length of thread, roll half onto a No-Tangle bobbin. Leave an 8" (20.5 cm) tail on either end of the rope for assembly later.

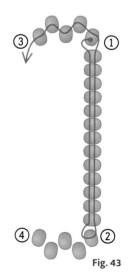

③ ①
④ ②

Fig. 43

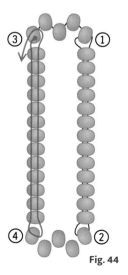

③ ①
④ ②

Fig. 44

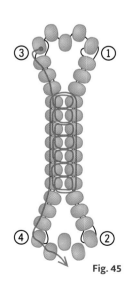

③ ①
④ ②

Fig. 45

TIP

Add thread by weaving through the CRAW sides following the thread path, circling around without having to tie half-hitch knots. Secure the tail threads in the same fashion.

...ODING THE RIVOLI SNAP CLOSURE

Repeat Steps 36–40 as in Adding the
...voli Bail Accent section but leave a 16"
...0.5 cm) tail when beginning to bead.
...o not secure the tail thread because it
...ll be used to attach the snap. String 3D,
...en pass through the next B added in the
...evious step. String 1 pearl, then pass
...rough the next B (Fig. 46). Repeat these
...o sequences around the rivoli bezel six
...mes. Step up through the second D of
...e first picot added in this step.

The picots from Step 49 are secured
...the second round and locked into the
...itch." Follow the peyote-stitch thread
...th by alternating between Round 1
...d Round 2 to secure the center picot
...ad. Repeat around six times. Then
...ss through Round 3 for assembly
...er (Fig. 47).

Use the tail thread to connect the
...ale part of the snap closure. Because
...ere are 14D and four openings on the
...ap, attachments are made at Locations
...2, 3, and 4. Pass through 1D, under
...e snap and over to the opposite end
...the original D (from bottom up).
...epeat the connection twice. Following
...e peyote-stitch thread path, pass to
...e C and the subsequent D. Repeat the
...nnection at this location through the
...me opening. Skip 1D. Proceed connect-
...g the second opening in the same way
...rough the next 2D. Skip 2D. Complete
...e remaining connections through the
...st two openings to mirror the first four
...nnections. Secure the tail thread and
...m (Figs. 48 and 49).

With a 36" (91.5 cm) length of
...read, string 16A and join into a
...ng with a square knot, leaving an 8"
...0.5 cm) tail. Pass through 1A away
...om the knot (Fig. 50).

ROUNDS 1–3: Begin circular peyote
...itch. String 1A, skip 1A on the ring,
...d pass through the next A. Repeat
...ven more times. Step up through the
...st A added in this round (Fig. 51).

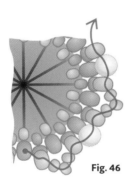

Fig. 46

Fig. 47

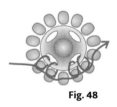

Fig. 48

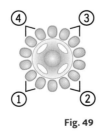

Fig. 49

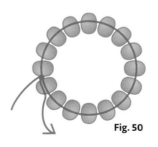

Fig. 50

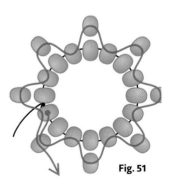

Fig. 51

54 ROUND 4: String 3D, then pass through the next A from Round 3. Repeat seven more times. Pass through all beads added again to stiffen the beadwork (**Fig. 52**).

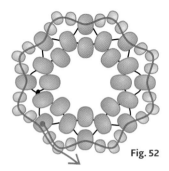

Fig. 52

55 Pass through to Round 2 to connect the female portion of the snap closure. Because there are 8A in Round 2, each snap opening will be connected to two consecutive As of that round. Attachments are made at Locations 1, 2, 3, and 4. Pass through 1A on Round 2 under the snap and over into the opposite end of the original A (from bottom up) as in Step 51. Repeat the connection twice. Following the peyote-stitch thread path, pass through the A on Round 3 and then back to the subsequent A of Round 2. Repeat the connection at this location through the same opening on the snap. Proceed connecting the subsequent As on Round 2 at Locations 2, 3, and 4. Pass through to the closest center bead of a 3-bead picot. Set aside the working thread for assembly later (**Fig. 53**).

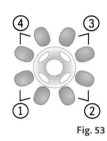

Fig. 53

56 With the tail thread, string 1C and pass through each A of Round 1. There should be 8C added. Step up through the first C added in this step (**Fig. 54**).

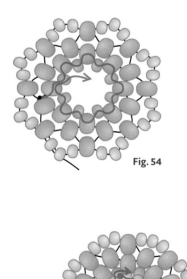

Fig. 54

57 String 1 pearl. Pass through the opposite-facing D (4C away). Pass back through the pearl and the opposite end of the original D. Following the peyote-stitch thread path, pass through the A of Round 1 and the subsequent C (**Fig. 55**).

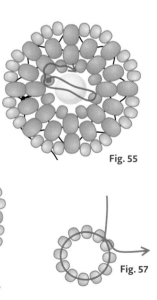

Fig. 55

58 Create a bezel around the pearl accent. String 3D, skip the next C, and pass through the Cs two beads away. Repeat around three times. Secure the tail and trim (**Fig. 56**).

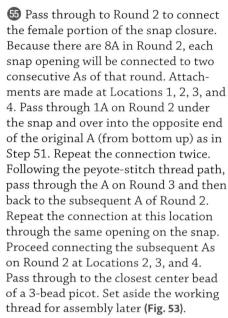

Fig. 56

MAKING THE SQUARE-STITCHED CONNECTION RINGS

59 With a 15" (38 cm) length of thread, string 12D and join into a ring with a square knot, leaving a 6" (15 cm) tail. Pass through 1D away from the knot (**Fig. 57**).

60 Square-stitch another set of 12D alongside the original ring to create a more substantial connection ring. String 1D, then pass through the original D of the ring and the next D. Repeat around eleven times (**Fig. 58**).

61 Pass through the first D added in Step 60 following the thread path. Secure and circle around all beads added in Step 60 to join the square stitches into a ring. Repeat around and secure the thread with several half-hitch knots (**Fig. 59**). Repeat with tail thread on the original ring. Secure the thread and trim.

62 Repeat Steps 59–61 to create two more connection rings.

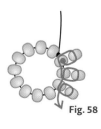

Fig. 57

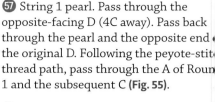

Fig. 58

Fig. 59

CONNECTING IT ALL TOGETHER

CONNECTING BAIL TO DROP: With
one of the connection rings, the bail will
be connected to the drop. Refer to **Fig. 35**
for the location on the drop and **Fig. 45**
for the location on the bail. On the drop,
string 1A. Pass through the A of the
CRAW edge. String 8D and the ring. Pass
through the original A on the drop again.
Reinforce through all beads added twice.
Secure the thread and trim. On the bail,
string 1A, then pass through the A of the
CRAW edge. String 8D and the ring. Pass
through the original A on the bail. Reinforce by passing through all beads added
twice. Secure the thread and trim.

**CONNECTING RING TO RIVOLI SNAP
(MALE):** Refer to **Fig. 47**. The rivoli bail
bead is positioned to connect to the
ring from Round 3. String 8D and a
second ring. Pass back through in the
opposite direction of the A from the
original A. Following the peyote-stitch
thread path, reinforce through all beads
added twice. Secure the thread and trim.

**CONNECTING RING TO SNAP
(FEMALE):** Refer to Step 55 where the
thread was woven to the second D of a
3-bead picot on the outer edge. *(Note:
These picots are flatter in appearance than
usual due to the distance between the As.)*

String 8D and the last ring. Pass through
the adjacent second D picot bead in the
opposite direction of the 3-bead picot.
Reinforce through all beads added twice.
Secure the thread and trim.

66 Connecting Ring to CRAW Rope:
String rope through the loop from
the Rivoli Bail Accent. String 1A, 1
fire-polished round, 8D, and the ring
attached to the Rivoli Snap (male). Pass
back through the fire-polished round,
the A, and the opposite-facing A on the
CRAW rope. Reinforce by repeating the
entire thread path twice. Secure the
thread through the CRAW rope and trim.
Repeat to connect the other side of the
rope to the last ring from the female
snap. Secure the thread through the
CRAW rope and trim (**Fig. 60**).

Fig. 60

TECHNIQUES

Circular peyote stitch

Herringbone stitch

Twisted tubular herringbone stitch

St. Petersburg stitch

Fringe

Right-angle weave

Netting

Ladder

Stitch-in-the-ditch embellishment

Picot

Zipping

MATERIALS

g purple-lined amethyst 11° Japanese seed beads (A)

.5 g copper 11° Japanese seed beads (B)

5 g raspberry bronze iris 11° Japanese seed beads (C)

6.5 g lavender blue gold luster 11° Japanese seed beads (D)

5 g opaque lavender 11° Japanese seed beads (E)

3 g purple-lined amethyst 15° Japanese seed beads (F)

7 g copper 15° Japanese seed beads (G)

3.5 g raspberry bronze iris 15° Japanese seed beads (H)

3 g lavender blue gold luster 15° Japanese seed beads (J)

1 light vitrail 16mm rivoli rhinestone

6 powder rose 4mm crystal pearls

34 amethyst 2mm Czech glass pearls

6 opaque amethyst luster 4mm fire-polished glass rounds

6 stone pink luster 4mm fire-polished glass rounds

6 iris 2.5×6mm pressed-glass rice drops

6 antique red luster 2.5×6mm pressed-glass rice drops

6 lila vega luster 2.5×6mm pressed-glass rice drops

28" (71 cm) of black 2mm rubber cord

Smoke 6 lb braided beading thread

TOOLS

Size 12 beading needles

Ruler

Scissors

SIZE
36½" (92.5 cm)

LEVEL
Advanced

KAYLA
LARIAT

My favorite color to design with is purple. The slider component of this twisted herringbone necklace is similar to the Rivoli Scallop Chain Earrings (page 40) and the Chrysanthemum Brooch (page 44) but with additional embellishments. The St. Petersburg leaves look like the leaves from *Bead Romantique* but are easier to create in one piece instead of two.

CREATING THE SLIDER

1 With a 60" (152.4 cm) length of thread, string 36A and join into a ring with a square knot, leaving an 8" (20.5 cm) tail. Pass through 1A away from the knot.

2 **ROUNDS 1–3:** Begin circular peyote stitch. String 1A, skip 1A on the ring, and pass through the next A. Repeat seventeen times. Step up through the first A added in this round.

ROUNDS 4–5: Work circular peyote stitch with 1A. Step up through the first A added in the respective round.

ROUNDS 6–7: Work circular peyote stitch with 1F. Step up through the first F added in the respective round.

ROUND 8: Work circular peyote stitch with 1G. Step up through the first G added in this round **(Fig. 1)**.

3 Insert the rivoli facedown into the bezel just created. The first round of peyote will then be facing up.

4 **ROUND 9:** Using the tail thread, work circular peyote stitch with 1F into the As from Round 1. Step up through the first F added in this round.

ROUND 10: Work circular peyote stitch with 1F. Step up through the first F added in this round.

ROUND 11: Work circular peyote stitch with 1G. Step up through the first G added in this round **(Fig. 2)**.

5 Flip the beadwork to the front. Pass through the 1A on Round 5 and stitch-in-the-ditch with a B passing through every A from Round 5. Step up through the first B added in this round **(Fig. 3)**.

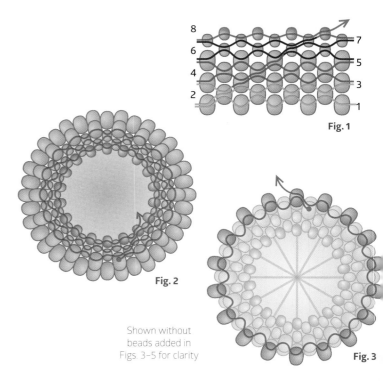

Fig. 1

Fig. 2

Shown without beads added in Figs. 3–5 for clarity

Fig. 3

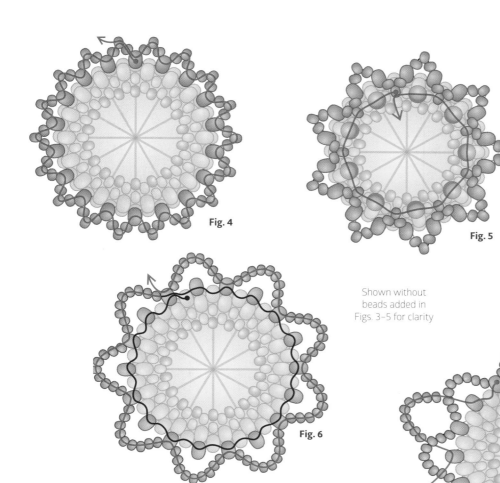

Fig. 4

Fig. 5

Shown without
beads added in
Figs. 3–5 for clarity

Fig. 6

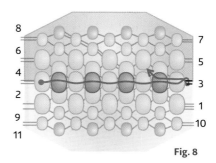

Fig. 7

● String 3G and pass through the next ⬤ added in Step 5. Repeat seventeen ⬤nes to create a picot edging. Step up ⬤rough 2G of the first picot (Fig. 4).

● String one 2mm pearl and pass back ⬤rough the second G of the next picot. ⬤peat around eight times to add a total ⬤ nine pearls. Reinforce by repeating the ⬤read path (Fig. 5).

● Following the thread path, pass ⬤rough 1A on Round 4 and stitch-in-⬤e-ditch with 1A passing through each ⬤on Round 4. Step up through the first ⬤added in this round (Fig. 6, blue thread).

● String 9H, skip the next A added in ⬤ep 8, and pass through the follow-⬤g third A. Repeat around, stringing ⬤H, skipping the next A of Step 8, and ⬤ssing through the following A seven ⬤nes. Reinforce and align the beadwork

by passing through all the beads added (Fig. 6, red thread).

🔟 Pass through the A from Round 4 and the second A from Step 8. String 9H above the first picot and pass under the second picot from Step 9 to the fourth A from Step 8. Repeat around nine times. Reinforce and align the bead-work by passing through all the beads added (Fig. 7).

⓫ Following the thread path, pass through the 1A on Round 3 and stitch-in-the-ditch with 1B passing through an A on Round 3. Repeat four times to add 4B.

⓬ To turn the weaving direction, pass under the thread from a previous thread pass and tie a half-hitch knot. Pass back through the A from Round 3 and the last B added in Step 11 (Fig. 8).

Fig. 8

13 String 2A, 1B, and 2A. Pass through the original B and the first 2A **(Fig. 9)**.

14 String 1B and 2A. Pass back through the third B added in Step 11, the adjoining 2A from Step 13, and the three beads added in this step. Pass through the second B from Step 11 **(Fig. 10)**.

15 String 2A and 1B. Pass back through the adjoining 2A from Step 14, the second B from Step 11, and the first two beads added in this step **(Fig. 11, blue thread)**.

16 String 1B and 2A. Pass back through the first B from Step 11, the adjoining 2A from Step 15, and the B added in this step **(Fig. 11, red thread)**.

17 String 2A, 1B, and 2A. Pass back through the B from the first row and through all the beads added in this step. Pass back through the next B from the first row.

18 String 2A and 1B. Pass through the adjoining 2A from Step 17, the B from the first row, and the 2A added in this step.

19 String 1B and 2A. Pass back through the next B from the first row, the adjoining 2A from Step 18, and all the beads added in this step. Pass through the last B from the first row.

20 String 2A and 1B. Pass through the adjoining two As from Step 19, the last B from the first row, and all the beads added in this step **(Fig. 12)**.

21 Repeat Steps 13–20 twice to create six rounds of the right-angle-weave band.

22 Zip the sixth row to the opposite side of the rivoli bezel. Align the band so there are 4A separating the connections. Pass through the seventh A on Round 3 from the last B added in Step 11 **(Fig. 13)**.

23 Pass through the second B from the band, the eighth A on Round 3, the third B from the band, the ninth A on Round 3, the last B from the band, and the tenth A on Round 3.

24 To turn the weaving direction, pass under the thread from a previous thread pass and tie a half-hitch knot. Pass back through the first B from the band.

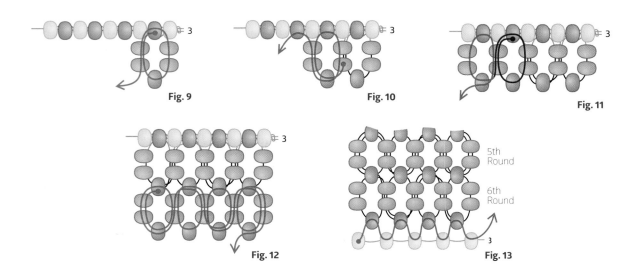

Fig. 9

Fig. 10

Fig. 11

Fig. 12

Fig. 13

5th Round

6th Round

Pass back through the 2A on the edge of the sixth row of the band. String 1F and pass through the 2A on the edge of the fifth row of the band. Repeat, stringing 1F and passing through each of the remaining 2A on the edge of the fourth, third, second, and first rows of the band. There should be 5F added on this edge. Add tension to the beadwork so the band is cinched inward to create the slider effect **(Fig. 14)**.

Pass thread through all beads connecting the band, exiting the last B. Turn the beadwork for better visibility and repeat Step 25 on the other side of the band. Secure the tail thread and trim.

FORMING THE BEADED BEAD

With an 18" (45.5 cm) length of thread, string a 2mm pearl and 3B. Join into a ring with a square knot, leaving 6" (15 cm) tail. Pass through the pearl and 1B.

String 2B and 1 pearl. Pass back through the adjoining B from Step 27 and the 2B added in this step **(Fig. 15)**.

String 1 pearl and 2B. Pass back through the adjoining B from Step 28, the pearl, and the B added in this step.

Repeat Steps 28–29 twice.

Repeat Step 28.

Join the beadwork into a ring. String pearl and pass through the first B. String 1B and pass through the last B added in Step 31 and the pearl **(Fig. 16)**.

Create the same nine right-angle-weave links on the opposite side of the pearls. String 3B. Pass through the pearl from Step 32 and the 3B added in this step **(Fig. 17, green thread)**.

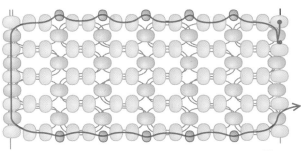

Fig. 14

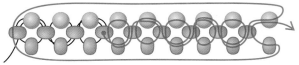

Fig. 15

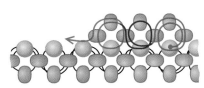

Fig. 16

Fig. 17

34 Pass back through the second pearl. String 2B and pass through the adjoining B from Step 33, the pearl, and the B added in this step **(Fig. 17, blue thread)**.

35 String 2B and pass back through the third pearl, the adjoining B, the 2B added in this step, and the fourth pearl **(Fig. 17, red thread)**.

36 Repeat Steps 34–35 twice.

37 Repeat Step 34.

38 Join the final connection by stringing 1B. Pass back through the adjoining B from Step 33, the last pearl, and the adjoining B from Step 37. Pass through the B added in this step, the adjoining B from Step 33, and the last pearl.

39 String 3H and pass through the next pearl. Repeat, stringing 3H and passing through each of the remaining eight pearls **(Fig. 18)**.

40 Following the thread path, pass back up through 2B of the top right-angle-weave link.

41 String 1G and pass through the next B of the second right-angle-weave link. Repeat, stringing 1G into each of the B from the remaining eight right-angle-weave links. Pass through this thread path and through the added beads again **(Fig. 19)**.

42 Following the thread path, pass through 1B and the pearl, then back through 2B to the bottom right-angle-weave edge.

43 Repeat Step 41. Secure the thread and trim.

44 Repeat Steps 27–43 to create a second beaded bead.

Fig. 20

Fig. 21

Fig. 22

CREATING THE ST. PETERSBURG RUSSIAN LEAVES

45 With a 24" (61 cm) length of thread, string 3H, 1C, and 1H. Pass back through the third bead strung, leaving a 6" (15 cm) tail **(Fig. 20)**.

46 String 1H, skip the second H, and pass through the first H. Reverse weaving direction **(Fig. 21)**.

47 String 1H and pass through the H added in Step 46 **(Fig. 22)**.

48 String 1H and pass through last H added in Step 45.

49 String 1H, 1C, and 1H. Pass back through the first H added in this step **(Fig. 23, green thread)**.

50 String 1H and peyote-stitch through the second H added in Step 47. Reverse weaving direction **(Fig. 23, blue thread)**.

Fig. 23

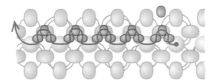
Fig. 18

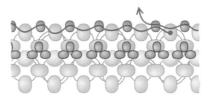
Fig. 19

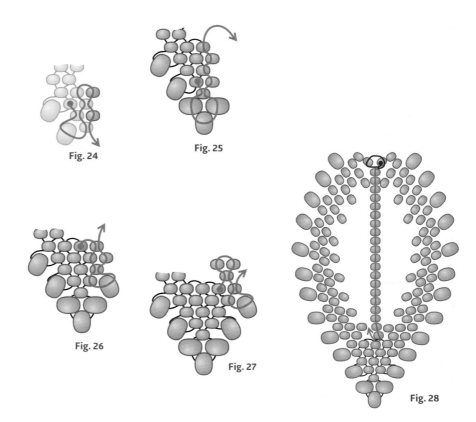

Fig. 24

Fig. 25

Fig. 26

Fig. 27

Fig. 28

51 String 1H and pass through the [added in Step 50.

52 String 1H and pass through the last [added in Step 49 (**Fig. 23, red thread**).

53 Repeat Steps 49–52 nine times. On the last repeat of Step 51, string 1G instead of 1H. The G marks the center of the vein on the bottom of the leaf (**Fig. 24**).

54 Create the leaf point. String 1H and [C. Pass back through the H.

55 String 1H and pass through the [added in the last repeat of Step 52.

56 String 1H and pass through the [. Reverse weaving direction (**Fig. 25**).

57 String 1H and pass through the [added in Step 56.

58 String 1H and pass through the [added in Step 55.

59 String 1C and pass through the [added in Step 58 (**Fig. 26**).

60 String 1H and pass through the [added in Step 57.

61 String 3H and pass through the [rst H.

62 String 1H and pass through the [added in Step 60.

63 String 1C and pass through the [added in Step 62 (**Fig. 27**).

64 Repeat Steps 60–63 nine times.

65 String 1H and pass through the second H added in the last repeat of Step 61.

66 Attach the two leaf sides and create the veins. Pass through the third H added in the last repeat of Step 61. To join, ladder-stitch to the complementary H on the opposite side of the leaf. Pass through the complementary H and back through the original H on the right side. String 20G and pass under the thread from a previous thread pass on the right side of the G marking the bottom of the leaf (**Fig. 28**).

Note: The veins will range from three to six 15° beads depending on your thread tension when you created the initial leaf sides. This is visually determined by how steep and round you want the leaf veins to appear in the final leaf. Generally, there are three or four beads on the bottom veins and up to six beads on the widest part of the leaf (**Fig. 29**).

67 **VEIN 1:** Pass back up through four of the 20G on the stem. String 3G and pass through the first inner H on the left side and back through the 3G.

VEIN 2: Pass up through 2G on the stem. String 4G and pass through the second inner H on the right side and back through the 4G. *Note: Each successive connection will be made through every other inner H, alternating from the left to the right side counting from the bottom up.*

VEIN 3: Pass up through 4G on the stem. String 6G and pass through the third inner H on the left side and back through the 6G.

VEIN 4: Pass up through 2G on the stem. String 6G and pass through the fourth inner H on the right side and back through the 6G.

VEIN 5: Pass up through 3G on the stem. String 6G and pass through the fifth inner H on the left side and back through the 6G.

VEIN 6: Pass up through 2G on the stem. String 6G and pass through the sixth inner H on the left side and back through the 6G. Pass up through the last 3G on the stem, into the last inner H on the left, and down through the adjacent H on the right side.

68 Reinforce and align the vein by weaving down the stem. Pass under the thread from a previous thread pass on the left side of the G marking the bottom of the leaf. Pass back through the stem. Secure the working thread and trim (**Fig. 30**).

69 With the tail thread, string 3H and pass through the opposite H on the right side. Secure the tail thread and trim. This creates a picot at the center top of the leaf for adding to the fringe later (**Fig. 31**).

70 Repeat Steps 50–84 five times to create six leaves made with C and H (Leaf A).

71 Repeat Steps 45–70 six times, substituting D for C and J for H, to create six leaves made with D and J (Leaf B).

72 Repeat Steps 45–70 six times, substituting A for C and F for H, to create six leaves made with A and F. (Leaf C).

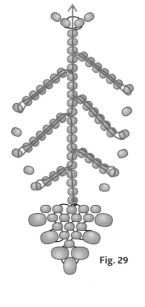

Fig. 29

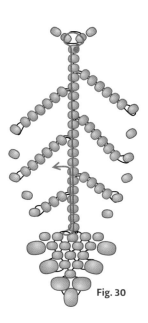

Fig. 30

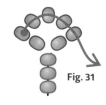

Fig. 31

CREATING THE TWISTED HERRINGBONE ROPE

73 **LADDER 1:** With a 60" (152.4 cm) length of thread, string 2B and 2D. Pass back through the 2B and 2D to create the first ladder stitch **(Fig. 32, orange thread)**.

LADDER 2: String 2B, then pass through the 2D and the 2B added in this step **(Fig. 32, green thread)**.

LADDER 3: String 2E, then pass through the 2B and the 2E added in this step **(Fig. 32, blue thread)**.

LADDER 4: String 2G, then pass through the 2E and the 2B added in this step.

LADDER 5: String 2A, then pass through the 2B and the 2A added in this step.

LADDER 6: Join into a ring by passing back through the first 2B of Ladder 1, through the 2A from Ladder 5, and back up through the first 2B of Ladder 1 **(Fig. 32, red thread)**.

74 Start a herringbone stitch round. String 1B and 1D. Pass down through 1D and up through the adjacent B. String 1B and 1E. Pass down through 1E and up through the adjacent B. String 1B and 1A, then pass down through 1A and up 2B to step up **(Fig. 33)**.

75 Repeat Step 74. This completes four rounds, two rounds of herringbone stitch and two rounds of ladder stitch. Insert the cord into the center of the tube and start building the rope around the cord.

76 On the fifth and successive rounds, the herringbone will start to twist. String 1B and 1D, then pass down through 1D and up through two adjacent Bs. String 1B and 1E, then pass down through 1E and up through two adjacent Bs. String 1B and 1A, then pass down through 1A and up through 3B to step up **(Fig. 34)**.

77 Repeat Step 76 until the rope measures 28" (71 cm). Follow the herringbone thread path and close up the end of rope around the cord. Secure the thread and trim.

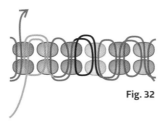

Fig. 32

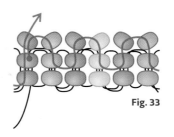

Fig. 33

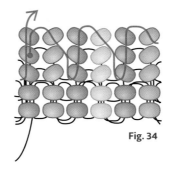

Fig. 34

The cord gives the necklace a nice weight and drape.

ASSEMBLING THE NECKLACE & ADDING FRINGE

78 String both ends of the rope through the slider component. Then slide the beaded beads onto each of the rope ends. *Note: Group the leaves and embellishment beads into six sets. Each side of the rope will have three fringes with alternating leaves and embellishments for visual interest.*

79 With a 60" (152.4 cm) length of thread, add thread through the Bs of the rope. Pass through several Bs, pass under the thread from a previous thread pass, and tie a half-hitch knot. Repeat twice until reaching the end of the rope.

80 String 45B and 2G. Pass through the center picot bead of Leaf A. String 2G and pass up through 1B on the stem **(Fig. 35)**.

81 String 3B, one 4mm pearl, and 3G. Pass back through the pearl and third B added in this step.

82 String 1B and 5G, then pass back through the fourth G. String 3G, then pass through the B added in this step and the second B from Step 81. Repeat this step and then pass through the first B from Step 81.

83 Pass up through 7B on the stem. String 3B, 2G, an iris pressed-glass rice drop, and 2G. Pass back up through the third B added in this step. Repeat Step 82 twice to create two mini leaves.

84 Pass up through 9B on the stem. String 3B and 2G. Pass through the center picot bead of Leaf B. String 2G, then pass back up through the third and second Bs added in this step.

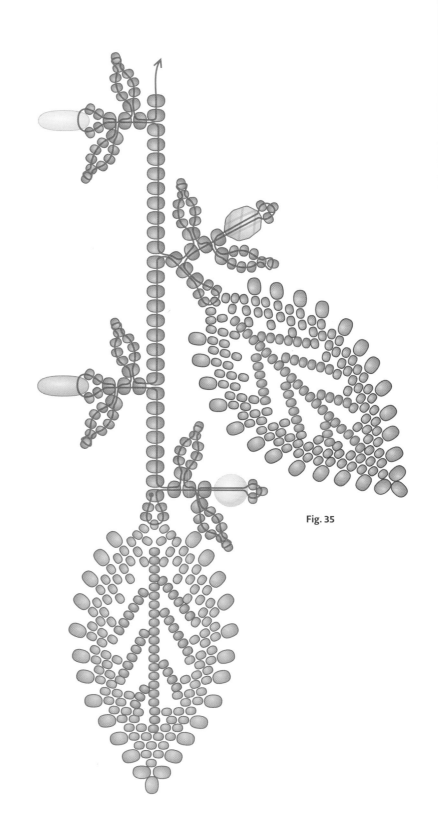

Fig. 35

85 String 3B, 1 opaque amethyst luster fire-polished round, and 3G. Pass back up through the fire-polished round and third B added in this step. Repeat Step 82 twice to create two mini leaves.

86 Pass up through 9B on the stem. String 3B, 2G, 1 lila vega pressed-glass rice drop, and 2G. Pass back up through the third B added in this step. Repeat Step 82 twice to create two mini leaves.

87 Pass up through 9B on the stem. String 3B and 2G, then pass through the center picot bead of Leaf C. String 2G, then pass through the third and second Bs added in this step.

88 String 3B, 1 stone pink luster fire-polished round, and 3G. Pass back up through the fire-polished round and the third B added in this step. Repeat Step 82 twice to create two mini leaves.

89 Pass up through 9B on the stem. String 3B, 2G, 1 antique red luster pressed-glass rice drop, and 2G. Pass back up through the third B added in this step. Repeat Step 82 twice to create two mini leaves.

90 Pass back down the stem to the Leaf A connection and then back up to strengthen and align the stem.

91 Repeat Steps 80–90 for a second and third fringe. Secure the thread through the rope and trim.

92 Repeat Steps 80–91 to add fringe to the other side of the lariat.

TIP

Changing the order of the components on each fringe creates a tiered effect and adds visual interest.

TREFOIL

EARRINGS

The trefoil is an ornamental design motif composed of three overlapping rings. It is prevalent in Gothic and Medieval architecture, especially in churches. I often design in threes because it symbolizes the number of completion, balance, and perfection. This design can be easily modified to four rings and converted to a quatrefoil.

CREATING THE FLOWERS

1 With a 15" (38 cm) length of thread, string 10D and join into a ring with a square knot, leaving an 8" (20.5 cm) tail **(Fig. 1, blue thread)**.

2 Using the tail thread, pass through the adjacent D. String 1 pearl, skip 4D, and pass through the fifth D. Pass through the pearl and the opposite side of the original D. Pass through the pearl again **(Fig. 1, red thread)**.

3 String 6B and pass through the opposite end of the pearl, circling one half of the pearl. String another 6B and pass through the opposite end of the pearl **(Fig. 2, blue thread)**.

4 Pass through the first 6B. String 1B. Pass through the second 6B and the first B strung in this step **(Fig. 2, red thread)**. *Note: There should be 13B circling the pearl.*

5 Begin square stitch. String 1C. Pass through the opposite end of the B and then through the next B.

6 Repeat Step 5 twelve more times, adding a total of 13C and creating the flower's stamen. On the last repeat, pass through all 13B circling the pearl again to align the stamens **(Fig. 3)**. *Note: There is no need to pass through the C stamen beads as you would in standard square stitch because we want them to be free-floating.* Secure the thread and trim.

7 With the working thread, pass through the adjacent D, then pass up to the second (or upper hole) of the same D. String 1A and pass through the upper hole of the next D. Repeat nine times to add a total of 10D.

8 Pass through all beads in Step 7 again **(Fig. 4)**. Secure the thread and trim.

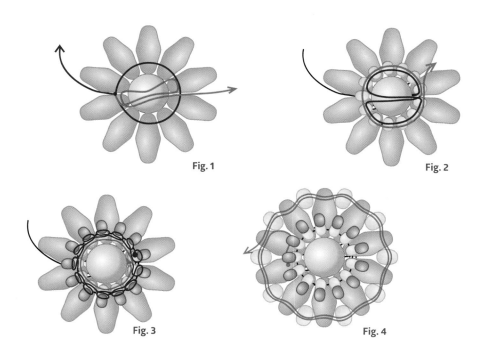

Fig. 1

Fig. 2

Fig. 3

Fig. 4

9 Repeat Steps 1–8 to create two more flowers. On one of the three flowers start with 24" (61 cm) of thread and leave the working thread untrimmed after Step 8 for assembly later.

JOINING THE FLOWERS TO CREATE THE TREFOIL

10 Using Flower 3 with the long (24" or 61 cm) working thread, pass the thread to an A. String 3B, the ear wire, and 2B. Pass through the A again to create a loop. Beading direction is viewed from the back of flower **(Fig. 5, green thread)**. Pass through all 5B again to reinforce the connection **(Fig. 5, blue thread)**. Continue to pass through 3A from the loop on Flower 1 **(Fig. 5, red thread)**.

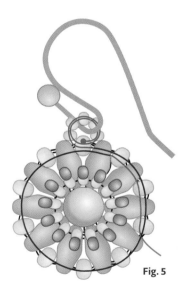

Fig. 5

11 String 1 bicone and pass back through the A on Flower 2. Pass back through the bicone and the A on Flower 1. Pass through the bicone and the A again on Flower 2 **(Fig. 6, turquoise thread)**.

12 Pass through the next D and the following A on Flower 2. Pass through the opposite-facing A on Flower 1 (this location is 4A to the right from the loop) and then pass through the A on Flower 2 again. Pass through the next D and the following A on Flower 2 **(Fig. 6, purple thread)**.

13 String 1C and pass through an A on Flower 3. String 1C and pass through the fifth A from the loop on Flower 1. String 1C and pass through the original A on Flower 2. Reinforce and pass through all beads in this step **(Fig. 6, orange thread)**.

14 Pass through the next D and the following A on Flower 2. Pass through the opposite-facing A on Flower 3 and then pass through the A on Flower 2 again **(Fig. 6, green thread)**.

15 Pass through the next D and the following A on Flower 2. String 1 bicone and pass through the opposite-facing A on Flower 3. Pass back through the bicone and through the A on Flower 2. **(Fig. 6, blue thread)**.

16 String 5B, the briolette, and 2B. Pass back through the third B. String 2B and pass up through the opposite-facing A on Flower 3. Pass through the bicone and the A on Flower 2. Reinforce and pass through all beads in this step, then pass back through the A on Flower 3 **(Fig. 6, red thread)**.

17 Pass back through 3A and 3D in Flower 3. Pass through the opposite-facing A on Flower 1 and then pass through the A again on Flower 3.

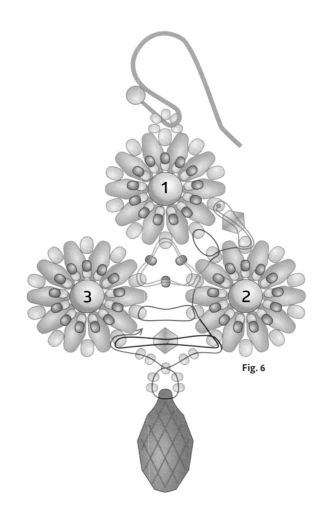

Fig. 6

18 Pass back through the next D and the following A on Flower 3. String 1 bicone and pass back through the opposite-facing A on Flower 1. Pass back through the bicone and through the A on Flower 3 **(Fig. 7)**. Secure the thread and trim.

19 Repeat Steps 1–18 for a second earring.

Fig. 7

↓ To create this variation, use blue iris matte 2-hole seed beads for D, gray pearls, cyclamen opal 13×6.5mm crystal drops, blue zircon 3mm bicones, dark silver seed beads for A and B, lavender blue gold luster seed beads for C, and sterling silver ear wires.

front

back

front

back

↑ To create this variation, use brown iris matte 2-hole seed beads for D, powder rose pearls, antique pink 13×6.5mm crystal drops, golden shadow 3mm bicones, bronze seed beads for A and B, gold-lined topaz AB seed beads for C, and gold-filled ear wires.

→ To create this variation, use rose-gold topaz luster 2-hole seed beads for D, bright gold pearls, astral pink 13×6.5mm crystal drops, padparadscha 3mm bicones, bronze seed beads for A and B, silver-lined gold AB seed beads for C, and gold-filled ear wires.

back

front

TECHNIQUES

Circular square stitch

Circular peyote stitch

Ladder stitch

MATERIALS

g bronze 11° Japanese seed beads (A)

g bronze 15° Japanese seed beads (B)

5 g gold-lined topaz AB 15° Japanese seed beads (C)

0 g brown iris matte 2.5×5mm -hole seed beads (D)

4 powder rose mm crystal pearls

8 powder rose 3mm crystal pearls

24 jonquil satin 3mm crystal bicones

11 light Colorado topaz 6.5mm gold-plated sliders

1 gold-plated 4-strand 26×6mm round tube clasp

Smoke 6 lb braided beading thread

TOOLS

Size 12 beading needles

Scissors

SIZE

7½" (19 cm)

LEVEL

Intermediate

CATHERINE
BRACELET

Catherine of Aragon was Queen of England and the wife of King Henry VIII. Inspired by the Tudors and jewelry of that period, I romanced the SuperDuos, two-hole seed beads, into miniature floral medallions and then joined them with Swarovski sew-on sliders. These versatile components can be easily modified to large medallions by adding more rounds of SuperDuos.

TIPS

→ This bracelet would also look lovely converted to a choker with an adjustable-length clasp.

→ You can substitute Pressed Twins in place of SuperDuos.

→ Create earrings or a pendant using four of the flower blossoms and embellish with any type of drop (i.e., crystal, fire-polished, glass, gemstone, etc.).

CREATING THE FLOWER BLOSSOM

1 With a 15" (38 cm) length of thread, string 10D and join into a ring with a square knot, leaving an 8" (20.5 cm) tail **(Fig. 1)**.

2 Using the tail thread, pass through the adjacent D. String a 4mm pearl, skip 4D, and pass through the fifth D. Pass back through the pearl and the opposite end of the original D. Pass through the pearl again **(Fig. 2)**.

3 String 6B and pass through the opposite end of the pearl, circling one half of the pearl. String another 6B and pass through the opposite end of the pearl **(Fig. 3a, blue thread)**.

4 Pass through the first 6B. String 1B to join the second set of 6B. *Note: There should be 13B circling the pearl.* Pass through the first B strung in this step **(Fig. 3a, red thread)**.

5 String 1C and pass through the opposite end of the B. Pass through the next B.

6 Repeat Step 5 twelve times, adding a total of 13C and creating the flower's stamen. On the last repeat, pass through all 13B circling the pearl again to align the stamens. Secure the tail thread and trim **(Fig. 3b)**.

7 With the working thread, pass through the adjacent D, then pass up to the second (or upper hole) of the same D. String 1A and pass through the upper hole of the next D. Repeat, adding 1A to each of the Ds nine times.

8 Pass through all beads in Step 7 again. Secure the thread and trim **(Fig. 4)**.

9 Repeat Steps 1–8 to create twenty-three more flower blossoms.

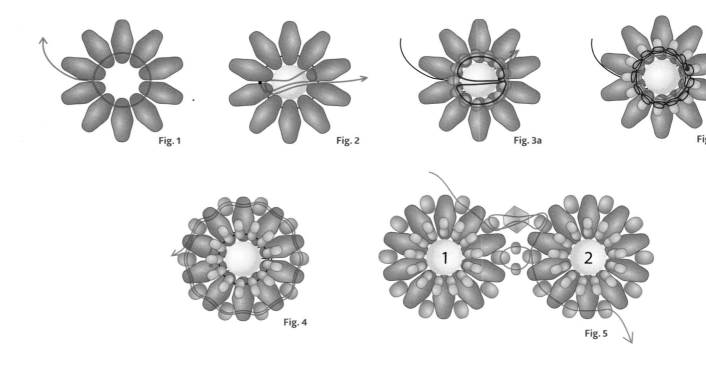

Fig. 1

Fig. 2

Fig. 3a

Fig. 3b

Fig. 4

Fig. 5

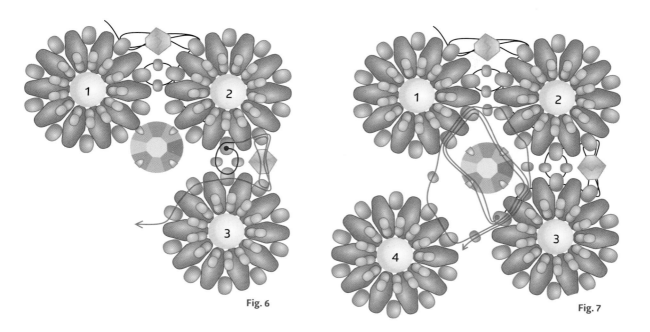

Fig. 6

Fig. 7

JOINING THE FLOWER BLOSSOMS

With a 60" (152.4 cm) length of thread, pass through 1A, 1D, and 1A on Flower 1, leaving a 12" (30.5 cm) tail. String 1 bicone and pass through 1A of Flower 2. Pass back through the bicone and the original A on Flower 1. Reinforce this connection by passing through the bicone and through the A on Flower 2.

Pass through the adjacent 1D and the next A. String 1B and pass through the opposite-facing A on Flower 1. String B, then pass back through the A on Flower 2.

Pass through the adjacent 1D, 1A, 1D, 1A, 1D, and 1A. This location is 3A from the connection created in Step 11 on Flower 2 (Fig. 5).

String 1B and pass through 1A of Flower 3. String 1B and pass through the A on Flower 2 again (Fig. 6, blue thread).

Pass through 1D and 1A on Flower. String 1 bicone and pass through the opposite-facing A on Flower 3. Pass back through the bicone and the A on Flower. Pass back through the bicone and back through the A on Flower 3.

⑮ Pass back through the adjacent 1D, 1A, 1D, 1A, 1D, and 1A. This location is 3A from the connection created in Step 14 on Flower 3 (Fig. 6, red thread).

⑯ The slider has two parallel holes. Pass through the left hole and back through the A two away from the connection created in Step 11. Pass through the D and the next A. Pass through the other hole on the slider and pass back through the A one away from the connection created in Step 13. Reinforce the slider connection by passing through this thread path again. Pass back through the 1D and 1A on Flower 3.

⑰ String 1B and pass back through 1A, 1D, and 1A on Flower 4. String 1B and pass through the beads (1A, 1D, and 1A) connecting Flower 1 to the slider. String 1B and pass through the A one away from the connection created in Step 11. Pass through 1D and 1A on Flower 2.

⑱ String 1B and pass through the beads (1A, 1D, and 1A) connecting Flower 3 to the slider. Pass through the first B added in Step 17 (Fig. 7).

FORMING THE BEZEL AROUND THE SLIDER

19 String 1A and pass back through the B. String 5B and pass through the next B at the corner of the slider. *String 1A and pass through the B. String 5B and pass through the next B at the corner of the slider. Repeat from *. String 1A and pass back through the third B. String 5B and pass through the last B at the corner of the slider. There should be 1A added on each of the corners with a 5B bezel setting on each side of the slider **(Fig. 8)**. Reinforce the bezel by passing through the thread path again.

20 Pass through 1A, 1D, 1A, 1D, and 1A on Flower 4. String 1B and pass through the opposite-facing A on Flower 1. String 1B and pass back through the A on Flower 4.

21 Pass back through 1D and 1A on Flower 4. String 1 bicone and pass through the opposite-facing A on Flower 1. Pass back through the bicone and the A on Flower 4. Pass through the bicone again and the A on Flower 1 **(Fig. 9)**.

22 To set up for adding Flower 5, pass through 1D, 1A, 1D, 1A, 1D, and 1A on Flower 1. Pass through 1B at the corner of the slider bezel, then through 1A, 1D, and 1A of Flower 2. Pass through 1B at the next corner of the slider bezel, then through 1A, 1D, 1A, 1D, 1A, 1D, 1A, 1D, and 1A of Flower 3 **(Fig. 10)**.

23 Repeat Steps 13–22 ten more times to join the remaining flowers.

24 For the center connection between Flower 23 and Flower 24, on the last repeat of Step 22, at the end, pass through 1A, 1D, 1A, 1D, and 1A of Flower 23 instead **(Fig. 11)**.

25 String 1B and pass through the adjacent A on Flower 24. String 1B and pass back through the A on Flower 23. Pass through 1D and 1A.

26 String 1 bicone and pass through the opposite-facing A on Flower 24. Pass back through the bicone and 1A on Flower 23. Pass back through 1D and 1A **(Fig. 11)**.

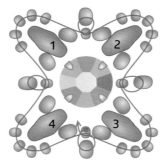

Fig. 8

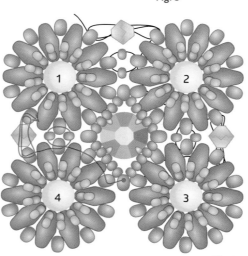

Fig. 9

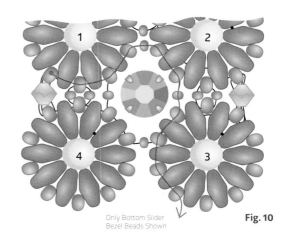

Only Bottom Slider Bezel Beads Shown

Fig. 10

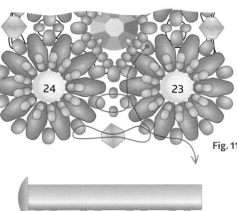

Fig. 11

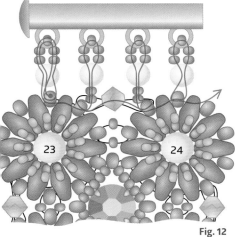

Fig. 12

CONNECTING THE TUBE CLASP

27 String one 3mm pearl and 5B. Pass through the outer loop on the tube clasp. Pass back through the pearl and the opposite end of the A on Flower 23. Reinforce this connection by passing through all beads added in this step, then pass through 1D and 1A (**Fig. 12**).

28 String 2B, one 3mm pearl, and 5B. Pass through the second loop on the tube clasp. Pass back through the pearl, 2B, and 1A. Reinforce this connection by passing through all the beads added in this step, then pass back through the adjacent A of Flower 24.

29 Repeat Step 28. Pass through 1D and 1A.

30 Repeat Step 27. Secure the thread and trim.

31 Repeat Steps 27–30 to connect the other side of the tube clasp.

{ VARIATIONS }

↓ To create this variation, use cream rose pearls, light peach bicones, light rose-gold–plated sliders, and ultra green luster matte 2-hole seed beads for D. Use the same seed beads as the main project colorway for A, B, and C.

↑ To create this variation, use platinum pearls, topaz bicones, aqua gold-plated sliders, and blue turquoise Senegal or blue turquoise bronze Picasso 2-hole seed beads for D. Use the same seed beads as the main project colorway for A, B, and C.

TECHNIQUES

Circular square stitch

Circular peyote stitch

Netting

Reverse picot

St. Petersburg stitch

MATERIALS

5 g purple iris 11° Japanese seed beads (A)

5 g brown iris 11° Japanese seed beads (B)

3 g bronze 11° Japanese seed beads (C)

3 g purple iris 15° Japanese seed beads (D)

2 g brown iris 15° Japanese seed beads (E)

3 g bronze 15° Japanese seed beads (F)

0.5 g gold-lined topaz AB 15° Japanese seed beads (G)

g brown iris matte .5×5mm 2-hole eed beads (H)

light vitrail 16mm voli rhinestone

light vitrail 4mm rivoli hinestones

5 light vitrail 12mm rivoli rhinestones

1 vintage gold 6mm crystal pearl

4 vintage gold 4mm crystal pearls

9 vintage gold 3mm crystal pearls

1 cyclamen opal 13×6.5mm briolette drop

2 cyclamen opal 11×5.5mm briolette drops

52 cyclamen opal 3mm crystal bicones

164 brown iris 3mm fire-polished glass rounds

16 amethyst luster 3mm fire-polished rounds

1 gold-plated 2-strand 16×6mm round tube clasp

Smoke 6 lb braided beading thread

TOOLS

Size 12 beading needles

Scissors

SIZE

19.5" (49.5 cm)

LEVEL

Advanced

CATHERINE
NECKLACE

Evoking the splendor that was the Tudor period, this regal design romances the SuperDuo (two-hole seed beads) to create small domes that capture a treasured gemstone. A quadruple St. Petersburg–stitched necklace adds the versatility of wearing this necklace in the more sparkly reverse side.

CREATING THE LARGE MEDALLION

1 With a 36" (91.5 cm) length of thread, string 12H and join into a ring with a square knot, leaving a 12" (30.5 cm) tail **(Fig. 1)**.

2 Using the tail thread, pass through the adjacent H. String one 6mm pearl, skip 5H, and pass through the sixth H. Pass back through the pearl and the opposite side of the original H. Pass through the pearl again **(Fig. 2)**.

3 String 10F and pass through the opposite end of the pearl, circling one half of the pearl. String another 10F and pass through the opposite end of the pearl **(Fig. 3)**.

4 Pass through the first 10F, the second 10F, and the first F added in Step 3.

5 String 1G and pass through the opposite end of the F. Pass through the next F.

6 Repeat Step 5 nineteen times, adding a total of 20G, creating the flower's stamen. On the last repeat, pass through all 20F circling the pearl again to align stamens. Secure the thread and trim **(Fig. 4)**.

7 With the working thread, pass through the adjacent H, then pass up to the second (or upper hole) of the same H. String 1C and pass through the upper hole of the next H **(Fig. 5, green thread)**. Repeat adding 1C to each of the Gs eleven times. Step up by passing through the first C added in this step **(Fig. 5, blue thread)**.

8 String 4D and pass through the next C **(Fig. 5, red thread)**. Repeat adding 4D to each of the Cs eleven times. Step up by passing through the first 3D added in this step.

9 String 3D and pass through the second and third Ds above the H to form reverse picots **(Fig. 6, blue thread)**.

10 String 1 bicone and pass through the second and third Cs above the H **(Fig. 6, red thread)**.

11 Repeat Steps 9–10 eleven times. Step up by passing through the first 2D added in Step 9.

12 String 3D and pass through the second D (or center bead) of each picot twelve times. Step up by passing through the first 3D added in this step **(Fig. 7)**. Flip the beadwork over to expose the domed empty cavity.

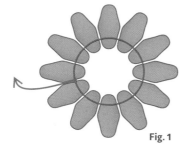

Fig. 1

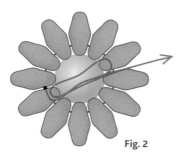

Fig. 2

Fig. 3

Fig. 4

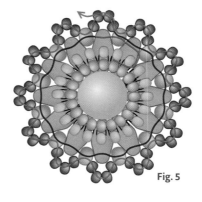

Fig. 5

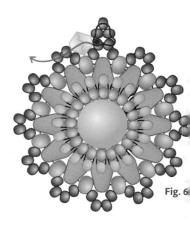

Fig. 6

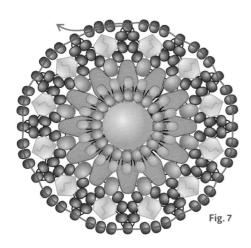

Fig. 7

Fig. 8

Repeat adding 1F into each set of 3D
ed from Step 12 twelve times. Step
by passing through the first F added
this step. Insert the 16mm rivoli face
(Fig. 8).

String 1F, 1C, and 1F through each
the Fs added in Step 13 twelve times.
p up by passing through the first F
d C added in this step **(Fig. 9)**.

String 1C and pass through each of
e Cs added in Step 14 twelve times. Pass
rough all beads added in this step again
tighten around the rivoli **(Fig. 10)**.

Following the thread path, pass thread
the second D (or center bead) of the
ot created in Steps 9–11. Pass down
e C and F from Step 14, the F from Step
, the 3D from Step 12, and through the
cond D from Step 11 **(Fig. 11)**.

String 1 brown iris fire-polished
und, 1C, and 1 brown iris fire-polished
und. Pass through the opposite end of
e same D, the next 3D from Step 12,
d through the second D from Step 11
g. 12)**.

Repeat Step 17 eleven times. On the
st repeat, circle around all beads added
ain. Flip the beadwork over.

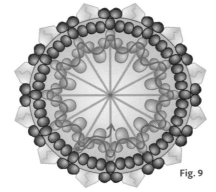

Fig. 9

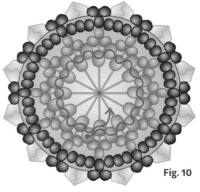

Fig. 10

19 To align the fire-polished round
embellishments from Steps 17–18,
pass through the bicone, the fire-polish
round, 1C, and the next fire-polished
round.

20 Repeat Step 19 eleven times. Set
aside the Large Medallion for assembly
later.

CREATING THE MEDIUM MEDALLION

*Note: Create the Medium Medallion
similarly to the Large Medallion. The main
differences are: A) There are ten of each
H, bicones, and paired fire-polished round
embellishments instead of twelve. B) There
are thirteen stamens instead of twenty
around the pearl. C) A 14mm rivoli is used
instead of a 16mm. D) There are ten repeats
of steps instead of twelve. E) A 4mm pearl*

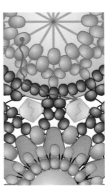

Fig. 11

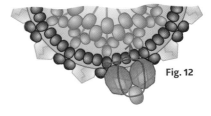

Fig. 12

is used instead of a 6mm. The steps are being repeated only to illustrate the differences.

21 With a 36" (91.5 cm) length of thread, string 10H and join into a ring with a square knot, leaving an 8" (20.5 cm) tail **(Fig. 13)**.

22 Using the tail thread, pass through the adjacent H. String one 4mm pearl, skip 4H, and pass through the fifth H. Pass back through the pearl and the opposite end of the H. Pass through the pearl again **(Fig. 14)**.

23 String 6F and pass through the opposite end of the pearl, circling one half of the pearl. String another 6F and pass through the opposite end of the pearl **(Fig. 15, blue thread)**.

24 Pass through the first 6F. String 1F. Pass through the second 6F and the first F added in this step **(Fig. 15, red thread)**.

25 String 1G and pass through the opposite end of the F. Pass through the next F.

26 Repeat Step 25 twelve times, adding a total of 13G and creating the flower's stamen **(Fig. 16, blue thread)**. On the last repeat, pass through all 13F circling the pearl again to align the stamens. Secure the thread and trim **(Fig. 16, red thread)**.

27 With the working thread, pass through the adjacent H and up to the second (or upper) hole of the same H. String 1C and pass through the upper hole of the next H. Repeat adding 1C to each of the Hs nine times. Step up by weaving through the first C added in this step **(Fig. 17)**.

28 Repeat Steps 8–20 from the Creating the Large Medallion section. Instead of twelve repeats of each step, there will be ten for the Medium Medallion. Use a 14mm rivoli instead of a 16mm one. Set aside for assembly later.

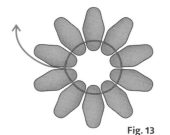
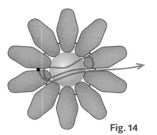
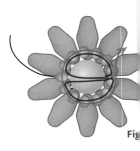

Fig. 13 — Fig. 14 — Fig.

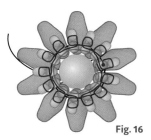
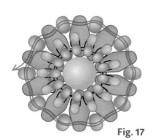

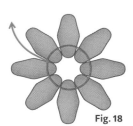
Fig. 16

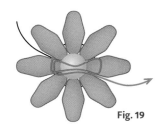
Fig. 17

29 Repeat Steps 21–28 to create three more Medium Medallions for a total of four Medium Medallions. Set aside for assembly later.

CREATING THE SMALL MEDALLION

30 With a 24" (61 cm) length of thread, string 8H and join into a ring with a square knot, leaving an 8" (20.5 cm) tail **(Fig. 18)**.

31 Using the tail thread, pass through the adjacent H. String one 3mm pearl, skip 3H, and pass through the fourth H. Pass back through the pearl and the opposite side of the H. Pass through the pearl again **(Fig. 19)**.

32 String 5F and pass through the opposite end of the pearl, circling one half of the pearl. String another 5F and pass through the opposite end of the pearl **(Fig. 20)**.

33 Pass through the first 5F, the second 5F, and the first F added in Step 31.

34 String 1G and pass through the opposite end of the F. Pass through the next F.

Fig. 18

Fig. 19

Fig. 20

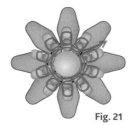

Fig. 21

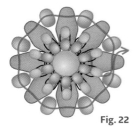

Fig. 22

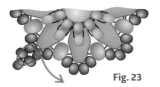

Fig. 23

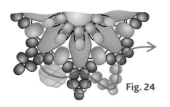

Fig. 24

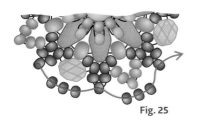

Fig. 25

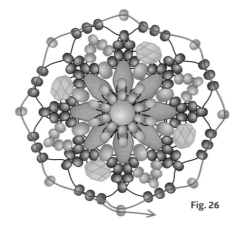

Fig. 26

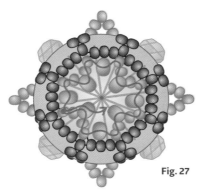

Fig. 27

35 Repeat Step 34 nine times, adding a total of 10G, creating the flower's stamen. On the last repeat, pass through all 10F circling the pearl again to align the stamens. Secure the thread and trim **(Fig. 21)**.

36 With the working thread, pass through the adjacent H and then pass up to the second (or upper) hole of the same H. String 1C and pass through the upper hole of the next H. Repeat adding 1C to each of the Hs seven more times. Step up by passing through the first C added in this step **(Fig. 22)**.

37 String 4D and pass through the next C. Repeat adding 4D to each of the Cs seven times. Step up by passing through the first 3D added in this step.

38 String 3D and pass through the second and third Ds above the H to form reverse picots **(Fig. 23)**.

39 String 1 amethyst luster fire-polished round and pass through the second and third Cs above the H.

40 Repeat Step 38.

41 String 5F and pass through the second and third Cs above the next H **(Fig. 24)**.

42 Repeat Steps 38–41 three times. Step up through the second D from Step 38.

43 String 3D and pass through the second D (or center bead) of the next picot. Repeat adding 3D to each of the center picot beads seven times. Step up by passing through the first 3D added in this step. Flip the beadwork over to reveal the domed, empty cavity **(Fig. 25)**.

44 String 1F, then pass through the next 3D. Repeat, adding 1F into each set of 3D from Step 43, seven times. Step up by passing through the first F added in this step. Insert the 12mm rivoli faceup **(Fig. 26)**.

45 String 1F, 1C, and 1F, then pass through the second F added in Step 44. String 1C and pass through the next F **(Fig. 27)**.

46 Repeat Step 45 three times. Pass through all beads added in this step again to tighten around the rivoli. Following the thread path, pass through to the center Fs of the picots created in Steps 41–42. Set aside for assembly later.

47 Repeat Steps 29–46 to create four more Small Medallions for a total of five Small Medallions. Set aside for assembly later. Connecting the Focal Medallion

48 On the Small Medallion 1, string 2F, a 13×6.5mm briolette, and 2F. Pass through the center F of the picot. Pass through all beads strung to reinforce the connection. Following the thread path, pass through the last 2F of this picot, the fire-polished round, the next 5F, the fire-polished round, and the first 3F of the picot opposite the connection made in this step **(Fig. 28)**.

49 **Fig. 29** illustrates the connection points on the focal medallion. Location 1: On the Large Medallion, string 2F and pass through the C between the fire-polished rounds on the Large Medallion. The weaving direction needs to switch, so pass under the thread from a previous thread pass. Pass back through the C, the 2F added in this step, and the third F of the picot on the Small Medallion 1 **(Fig. 30)**.

50 String 2F and pass through the adjacent C between the fire-polished rounds to the left of the connection made in Step 49. Pass under the thread from a previous thread pass. Pass back through the C, the 2F added in this step, the third F of the picot on the Small Medallion 1, the 2F added in Step 49, the original C, and the right fire-polished round **(Fig. 30)**.

51 **LOCATION 2:** Pass through 1 bicone, 1 fire-polished round, and 1C. String 6F, one 11×5.5mm briolette drop, and 2F. Pass through the third F of the picot on the Small Medallion 1. String 2F and pass through the next C, one away **(Fig. 31)**.

52 Pass under the thread from a previous thread pass. Pass back through the C, through all the beads added in Step 51 in reverse thread path, and through the original C. Pass under the thread from a previous thread pass. Pass back through the original C, the first 3F and the last 2F added in Step 51, the C, and the right fire-polished round.

53 **LOCATION 3:** Pass through 1 bicone, 1 fire-polished round, and 1C. String 2F

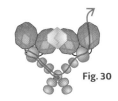

Fig. 30

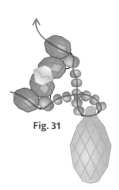

Fig. 31

Small Medallion 3

Small Medallion 2

Small Medallion 1

Fig. 29

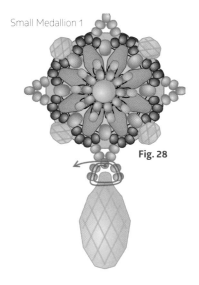

Small Medallion 1

Fig. 28

d pass through the third F of the picot, in Step 48, on the Small Medallion 2. ing 2F and pass through the next C, e away **(Fig. 32)**.

Pass under the thread from a pre-us thread pass. Pass back through C, 2F, the third F of the picot on the all Medallion 2, 2F, and the original Pass under the thread from a previ-s thread pass. Pass back through the ginal C, 2F, the third F of the picot on Small Medallion 2, 2F, the C, and the ht fire-polished round.

Pass through 1 bicone, the paired e-polished rounds (with its C in the ter), 1 bicone, the paired fire-polished nds (with its C in the center), 1 bi-ne, 1 fire-polished round, and 1 C.

LOCATION 4: Repeat Steps 53–54 h Small Medallion 3.

LOCATION 5: Pass through 1 bicone, re-polished round, and 1C. *Note:*

This connection mirrors that created in Steps 51–52. String 5F, one 11×5.5mm briolette, and 3F. Pass through the third F of the picot on the Small Medallion 3. String 2F and pass through the next C, one away **(Fig. 33)**.

58 Pass under the thread from a previous thread pass. Pass back through the C, through all the beads added in Step 57 in reverse thread path, and through the original C. Pass under the thread from a previous thread pass. Pass back through the original C, the first 3F and the last 2F added in Step 57, the C, and the right fire-polished round.

59 Secure the thread from all connected medallions and trim, except on Small Medallions 2 and 3.

CONNECTING THE REMAINING MEDALLIONS

60 Pass through to the third F of the picot on the Small Medallion 2, oppo-

site the connection made to the focal. Repeat Steps 49–50 to connect the Small Medallion 2 to the Medium Medallion 1. Secure the thread and trim.

61 On the Medium Medallion 1, pass through the fire-polished round and C, four paired fire-polished rounds away from the connection made in Step 60. Repeat Steps 53–54 to connect the Medium Medallion 1 to the Small Medallion 4. Secure the thread and trim.

62 Repeat Step 60 to connect the Small Medallion 3 to the Medium Medallion 2. Secure the thread and trim.

63 Repeat Steps 60–62 on the opposite side of the necklace to connect the Small Medallion 3 to the Medium Medallion 3, the Medium Medallion 3 to the Small Medallion 5, and the Small Medallion 5 to the Medium Medallion 4. Secure the thread and trim. Set aside for assembly later.

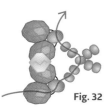

Fig. 32

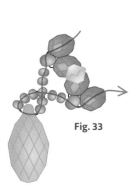

Fig. 33

CREATING THE TWO-COLORED QUADRUPLE ST. PETERSBURG STRAP

Note: The reversible quadruple St. Petersburg strap is first created as a single strap. Then another strap in the same color is added through the common center bead (in this case a 3mm fire-polished round). After creating a double St. Petersburg strap, a second color is introduced for the third and fourth straps added to the original strap through the common 3mm fire-polished round core bead. By flattening the straps, with one color on each side, a reversible two-color strap is created.

64 With a 60" (152.4 cm) length of thread, attach a stop bead by passing through the bead twice. Leave a 12" (30.5 cm) tail. String 6A, then pass back through the third and fourth As (creating a ladder stitch). Pull so the beads are aligned side by side **(Fig. 34)**.

65 String 3D and pass back through the fourth, third, and second As from Step 64 **(Fig. 35, blue thread)**.

66 String 1 brown iris fire-polished round and pass back through the sixth and fifth As from Step 64 **(Fig. 35, red thread)**.

67 String 4A and pass through the first and second As strung in this step **(Fig. 36, blue thread)**.

68 String 3D and pass back through the fourth and third As from Step 67 and the fifth A from Step 64.

69 String 1 brown iris fire-polished round and pass back through the fourth and third As from Step 67 **(Fig. 36, red thread)**.

70 Repeat Steps 67–69 twenty-eight times, until thirty fire-polished rounds have been added to the strap. The strap will measure about 15½" (39.5 cm). Set aside for assembly later.

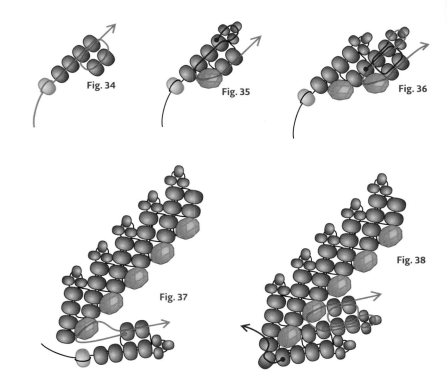

Fig. 34

Fig. 35

Fig. 36

Fig. 37

Fig. 38

71 With a 60" (152.4 cm) length of thread, repeat Steps 64–65 to create a second strap. Leave a 6" (15 cm) tail.

72 Pass up through the brown iris fire-polished round from Step 66 and through the sixth and fifth As from the second strap **(Fig. 37)**.

73 String 4A and pass through the first and second As strung in this step.

74 String 3D, then pass back through the fourth and third As from Step 73 and the fifth A from Step 71.

75 Pass up through the second brown iris fire-polished round on the core and through the sixth and fifth As from the second strap **(Fig. 38, red thread)**.

76 Repeat Steps 73–75 twenty-eight times. Secure the thread and trim. Remove the stop bead from the tail thread.

String 1A and pass through the first A on the first strap. Secure the thread and trim **(Fig. 38, blue thread)**.

77 Repeat Steps 71–76, substituting B for A, and E for D. Secure the thread and trim. Remove the stop bead from the ta thread, then secure the thread and trim

78 Repeat Step 77 to create another strap in the second color. Flatten the straps with your fingers so that one sid of the strap is in the main color (purple iris) and the other side of the strap is in the secondary color (brown iris).

79 Repeat Steps 64–78 to create another strap.

CONNECTING THE STRAP AND THE TUBE CLASP

Note: The main color side (purple iris) of the strap will be attached to the H side of the beadwork, while the secondary color side (brown iris) will be attached to the rivoli side of the beadwork.

80 With the main color side of the strap and H side of the beadwork facing up, make attachments through the center A added in Step 76. Remove the stop bead. Pass the tail thread from the first strap through the center A between the straps added in Step 76. String 2F and pass through the C at the center of the paired fire-polished rounds four counterclockwise away from the connection between Small Medallion 4 and Medium Medallion 2 **(Fig. 39)**.

81 Pass under the thread from a previous thread pass. Pass back through the C, 2F, and A between the two straps. String 2F and pass through the C, one away from the one in Step 80. Pass under the thread from a previous thread pass on the outside of the C.

82 String 2A, then pass through the second and first As on the first strap and back through the 2A just strung. String 3D, then pass back through the 2A, C, 2F, and center A between the two straps **(Fig. 40)**.

83 String 2A, then pass through the second and first As on the second strap and back through the 2A just strung. String 3D, then pass back through the 2A. Pass under the thread from a previous thread pass on the outside of the C between the two paired fire-polished rounds as in Step 80 **(Fig. 41)**.

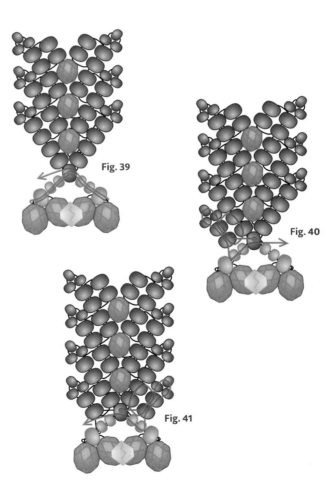

Fig. 39

Fig. 40

Fig. 41

84 Flip the beadwork over to connect the third and fourth straps to the Medium Medallion 2. The third strap will be to the left and the fourth strap to the right.

85 Repeat Steps 82–83, substituting B for A and E for D. Secure the thread and trim.

86 *Note: The opposite end of strap is connected to a two-ring tube clasp. The loops on the clasp are hidden between the strap beadwork.* Insert the tube clasp between the straps. Pass through the top ring on the tube clasp and into the opposite-facing B from the fourth strap. Pass back through the ring on the tube clasp and into the opposite end of the original A. Pass back through the B on the fourth strap. Flip the beadwork over to the other side **(Fig. 42)**.

87 String one 3mm pearl and pass through the opposite-facing top B on the third strap. Pass through the second ring on the tube clasp into the opposite-facing A from the second strap. Pass back through the ring on the tube clasp and through the original B again. Pass back through the A on the second strap. Flip the beadwork over to the other side **(Fig. 43)**.

88 String one 3mm pearl. Pass through the A on the first strap connected to the tube clasp and the first 2D of the picot **(Fig. 44)**.

89 String 1D, then pass through the second and first Es of the picot on the fourth strap, the B on the fourth strap connected to the tube clasp, and the pearl **(Fig. 45)**.

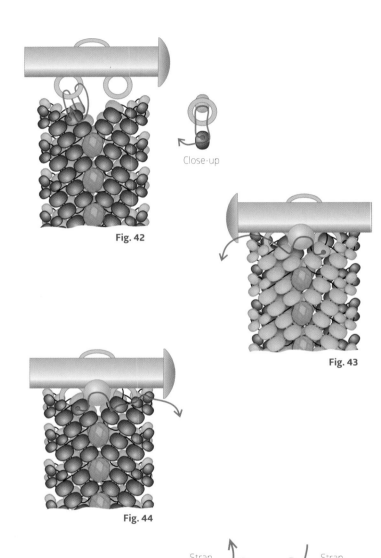

Close-up

Fig. 42

Fig. 43

Fig. 44

Strap 4   Strap 1

Fig. 45

90 String 3F and pass through the pearl again. Pass through the B connected to the tube clasp and the first 2E of the picot on the third strap **(Fig. 46)**.

91 Repeat Steps 89–90 **(Figs. 47 and 48)**.

92 Pass through the D on the side edge connecting the first strap to the fourth strap and through the second E (or center bead) of the picot on the fourth strap. String 2E and 1F. Pass through the pearl. String 1F and 2E, then pass through the second E (or center bead) of the picot on the third strap **(Fig. 49)**.

93 Repeat Step 92, substituting D for E. Secure the thread and trim.

94 Repeat Steps 80–93 to connect the other strap to the other side of the necklace.

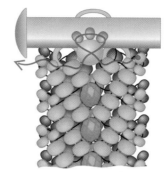

Fig. 46

Strap 3   Strap 4

Fig. 47

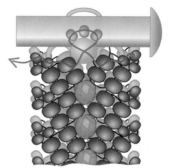

Fig. 48

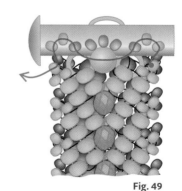

Fig. 49

TECHNIQUES

Square stitch

Circular peyote stitch

Circular right-angle weave

Reverse picot

Double reverse picot

Wrapped loop

Zipping

MATERIALS

0.5 g bronze-lined crystal 11° Japanese seed beads (A)

0.25 g bronze 11° Japanese seed beads (B)

0.5 g bronze-lined crystal 15° Japanese seed beads (C)

0.25 g bronze 15° Japanese seed beads (D)

8 golden shadow mm bicones

cream rose 6mm crystal pearls

2" (5 cm) of gold-filled 24-gauge wire

3" (7.5 cm) of gold-filled 1.2mm cable chain

1 pair of gold-plated lever-back ear wires

Smoke 6 lb braided beading thread

TOOLS

Size 12 beading needles

Round-nose pliers

Chain-nose pliers

Wire cutters

Ruler

Scissors

SIZE

2¼" (5.7 cm)

LEVEL

Beginner

CROWN JEWELS

EARRINGS

A crescent shape can be developed by just embellishing a portion of a Crown Jewels Necklace component. Chain is sewn and captured along the edge of the component, resulting in earrings full of fun movement and providing the "swing" to evoke a chandelier.

1 With 24" (61 cm) of thread, string 1 pearl and 7A. Pass through the opposite end of the pearl, leaving a 6" (15 cm) tail. String another 7A and pass through the opposite end of the pearl (**Fig. 1**).

2 Pass through the first 7A and string 1A. Pass through the second 7A and string 1A. Pass through the first A (**Fig. 2**).

3 String 1A, then pass through the original A again and the next A, circling the pearl (**Fig. 3**).

4 Repeat Step 3 fifteen more times. On the last repeat, pass back through the A just added, then through all fifteen beads and the first A. This creates a square-stitched bezel. Secure the tail thread through the bezel and trim. (**Fig. 4**).

5 String 1B, skip 1A, and pass through the next A on the lower bezel round.

6 Repeat Step 5 seven times for a total of 8B added. Step up by passing through the first B (**Fig. 5**).

7 String 1 bicone and pass through the next B. String 3C and pass through the same B again. String another 3C and

pass through the same B once more to create a reverse picot (**Fig. 6, blue thread**).

8 Repeat Step 7 six times.

9 String 1 bicone through the first A without adding the double reverse picot (**Fig. 6, red thread**).

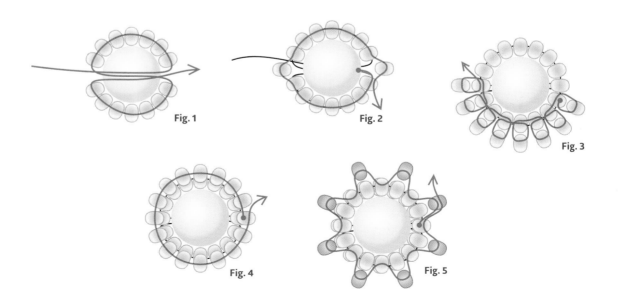

Fig. 1

Fig. 2

Fig. 3

Fig. 4

Fig. 5

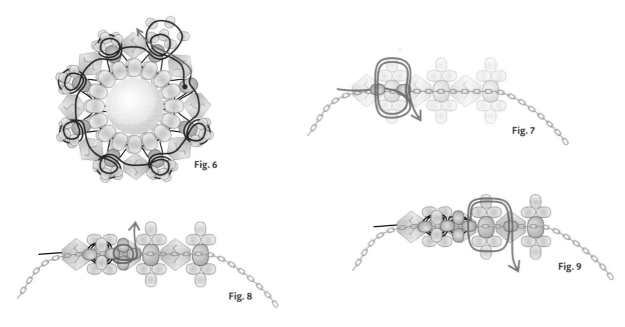

Fig. 6

Fig. 7

Fig. 8

Fig. 9

Insert the 3" (7.5 cm) chain in between the two picot embellishments you stitch the edge with right-angle weave. Leave about ¾" (2 cm) or about sixteen links of the chain tail uncaptured at the start.

Pass through the bicone, B, and the second C of the rear picot.

String 1D and pass through the second C of the front picot. String 1D and pass through the second C of the rear picot. Pass through all beads added and exit from the second D (Fig. 7).

String 3D and pass through the opposite end of the original D and the first 2D added in this step. The chain is being captured between the two picots with a right-angle-weave rolled edge. Use the edge to the back as you add right-angle-weave stitches so that the rolled edge does not collapse over the bicones (Fig. 8).

⑭ Pass through the second C of the next front picot. String 1D and pass through the second C of the rear picot, the second D strung in Step 13, the second C of the front picot, and the D added in this step (Fig. 9).

⑮ Repeat Steps 13–14 six times. Secure the thread and trim.

⑯ Measure the chain on each side to ensure it is ¾" (2 cm) or sixteen links long. Trim with wire cutters if necessary.

⑰ Create a ¹⁄₁₂" (2mm) loop with one end of the 2" (5 cm) wire. Insert the left chain and then the right chain. Ensure the chains are not twisted, then complete the wrapped loop. Insert 1 bicone and repeat, creating a ¹⁄₁₂" (2mm) wrapped loop on the other end (Fig. 10). String the loop through an open loop lever-back.

⑱ Repeat Steps 1–17 to create the other earring.

Fig. 10

{ TIP }

To ensure the chain is even on both sides, insert your needle through both chain ends.

BELLA FIORE

TECHNIQUES
Running stitch

Backstitch

Square stitch

Circular peyote stitch

Reverse picot

MATERIALS
0.40 g bronze-lined crystal 11° Japanese seed beads (A)

0.10 g bronze 11° Japanese seed beads (B)

0.75 g gold-lined aqua 11° Japanese seed beads (C)

0.10 g bronze-lined crystal 15° Japanese seed beads (D)

0.25 g gold-lined aqua 15° Japanese seed beads (E)

9 golden shadow 3mm crystal bicones

1 cream rose 6mm crystal pearl

12" (30.5 cm) of blushing bride 1½" (3.8 cm) hand-dyed silk bias ribbon

2" (5 cm) of chameleon ⅝" (1.5 cm) hand-dyed silk bias ribbon

36" (91.5 cm) of bella donna ½" (1.3 cm) hand-dyed silk tie

Cotton ball or scrap yarn

Smoke 6 lb braided beading thread

TOOLS
Size 12 beading needles

Ruler

Scissors

SIZE
Adjustable with 2¼" (5.7 cm) flower

LEVEL
Intermediate

I simply love Mother Nature's inspiration and often emulate floral motifs in my beadwork designs. *Bella fiore* is Italian for "beautiful flower." The flower focal, created with hand-dyed silk bias ribbons, can be worn in three ways: as a lariat, a pendant, or a wrap bracelet. Multiple-purpose jewelry expands your design options.

CREATING THE FLOWER

❶ With a 12" (30.5 cm) strip of 1½" (3.8 cm) silk bias ribbon, fold the ribbon at about ⅞" (2.2 cm) from one edge, so that the top layer is about two-thirds the width of the bottom layer. Anchor an 18" (45.5 cm) length of thread to the ribbon with a backstitch to secure. Start with the needle at the top of the ribbon ⅛" (3 mm) from the raw edge. Scoop up a little ribbon onto the needle, leaving about ¼" (6 mm) tail. Repeat backstitching twice and gently tug on the thread. Proceed with a running stitch down the cut edge, across the folded edge, and up the other cut edge as shown **(Fig. 1)**.

❷ Pull the thread so the ribbon gathers to reduce the length. Curl the gathered ribbon so it overlaps about ¼" (6 mm) and secure in place with backstitches as in Step 1. Join the two ends with several backstitches as in Step 1. Secure the thread and trim **(Figs. 2a and 2b)**.

TIP

Slide the ribbon onto the silk tie and wear as a pendant, a lariat, or a wrap bracelet. As a pendant, string the ends of the silk tie through the two loops and tie a bow at the back of the neck. You can adjust the length of your necklace easily. As a lariat, slide both ends of the silk tie into the slider and adjust the location of the flower as desired. As a wrap bracelet, center the flower on the silk tie and wrap around the wrist. Add a loose double overhand knot and hide the knot behind the wraps of ribbon.

Fig. 1

Fig. 2a

Fig. 2b

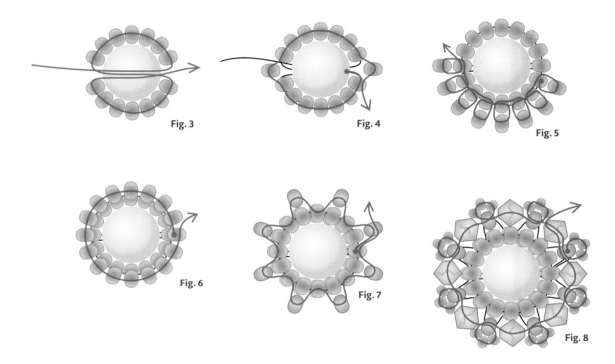

Fig. 3

Fig. 4

Fig. 5

Fig. 6

Fig. 7

Fig. 8

FORMING THE CENTER FLOWER EMBELLISHMENT

❸ With 24" (61 cm) of thread, string 1 pearl and 7A. Pass through the opposite end of the pearl, leaving a 6" (15 cm) tail. String another 7A and pass through the opposite end of the pearl **(Fig. 3)**.

❹ Pass through the first 7A again and string 1A. Pass through the second 7A and string 1A. Pass through the first A again from Step 3 **(Fig. 4)**.

❺ String 1A. Pass through the original A again and continue through the next A, circling the pearl. Repeat fifteen times **(Fig. 5)**.

❻ On the last repeat, pass through the A just added and then through all remaining fifteen beads from Step 5 and through the first A again. This creates a square-stitched bezel. Use the tail thread to reinforce and align the bezel by circling around the beads twice. Secure the thread in the bezel and trim **(Fig. 6)**.

❼ Begin peyote stitch by stringing 1B, skip 1A, and pass through the next A on the lower bezel round. There should be 8B added. Step up through the first B added in this step **(Fig. 7)**.

❽ String 1 bicone and pass through the next B around. String 3D and pass through the B again for a reverse picot. Repeat around seven times. Step up through the first bicone and B. Set aside for assembly later **(Fig. 8)**.

FINISHING THE BACK

9 Fold the ⅝" (1.5 cm) ribbon in half. *(Note: There is no front or back side to the ribbon.)* With 24" (61 cm) of thread, anchor the thread to the ribbon edge, joining the folded ribbon with a backstitch. Start at the lower right corner of the ribbon edge ⅛" (3 mm) from the raw edge. Scoop up a little ribbon onto the needle from both layers, leaving about ¼" (6 mm) tail **(Fig. 9a)**. Repeat backstitching twice and gently tug on the thread. Proceed with a running stitch as shown in **Fig. 9b**. Secure the end and lock the stitch in place with several backstitches. Flip the ribbon pocket inside out. Fill the cavity with a small bit of cotton from the cotton ball or use scrap yarn **(Fig. 9c)**. Proceed again with a running stitch **(Fig. 9d)**. Secure the thread and lock the stitches in place with several backstitches. Flatten the ribbon cushion with your fingers so the exposed stitches are centered **(Fig. 9e)**.

10 Flip the ribbon cushion over. Weave the needle to the edge. String 1C. Stitch through the fabric one bead space distance and back up through to the front of the C to create the first backstitch. Pass back through the C. Repeat twenty-seven more times for a total of twenty-eight beads. Step up by passing through the first C **(Fig. 10)**.

11 String 1C, skip 1C on the ring created from Step 10, and pass through the next C. Repeat thirteen more times. Step up by passing through the first C added in this round **(Fig. 11)**.

12 String 3E. Pass through the next C from Step 11. Repeat around thirteen more times. Step up by passing through the first 2E added in this round **(Fig. 12)**.

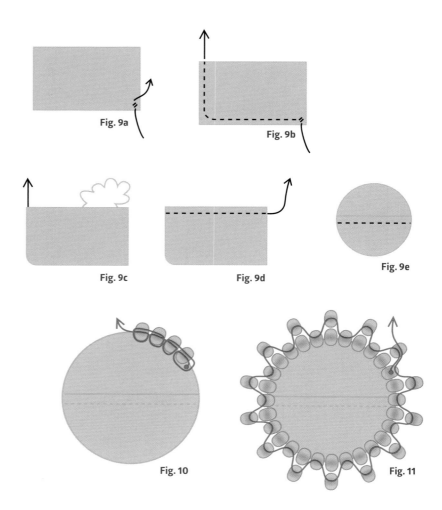

Fig. 9a

Fig. 9b

Fig. 9c

Fig. 9d

Fig. 9e

Fig. 10

Fig. 11

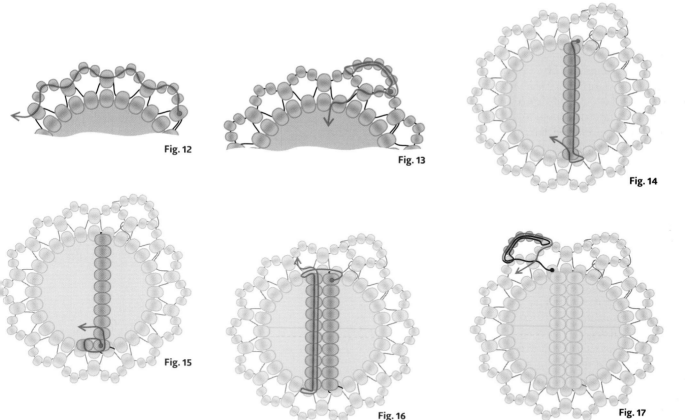

Fig. 12

Fig. 13

Fig. 14

Fig. 15

Fig. 16

Fig. 17

⑬ To create the pendant loops, string 5E and pass through the second E of the picot to the left. Pass back through the 5E just strung and then through the original E of the first picot. Reinforce the thread path once more. Pass back through the third E of the respective picot, the C of the third round, and through the C of the original ring from Step 10, following the peyote thread path **(Fig. 13)**.

⑭ String 10C and pass through the opposite C, seven picots clockwise away. Pass back through the last C strung in this step **(Fig. 14)**.

⑮ String 1C and pass back through the opposite end of the original C for the first square stitch. Pass through the next C from Step 14. Repeat square stitch nine more times **(Fig. 15)**.

⑯ Pass through the opposite end of the C from Step 13. Pass through the next 2C on the original ring and then through all 10C added from Step 15. Secure and align the slider to the C two beads clockwise from Step 15. Pass back through the 10C from Step 15 and through the opposite end of the C, two beads to the left of Step 15 **(Fig. 16)**.

⑰ Pass through the respective C from Step 11 and the first two E from Step 12, two picots counterclockwise away from the first loop created in Step 13. String 5E and pass through the second E of the next picot to the right **(Fig. 17, blue thread)**. Pass back in reverse direction through the 5E just strung and then through the opposite end of the E of the original picot in this step. Reinforce through the thread path once more. Pass counterclockwise to the closest C from Step 11 **(Fig. 17, red thread)**. Set aside for assembly later.

CONNECTING IT TOGETHER

18 Place the pearl embellishment at the center of the flower. The embellishment will be tacked onto the ribbon with backstitches through the Bs following the previous thread path. Pick up a small amount of ribbon with the needle and pass back through the opposite end of the original B from front to back. Pass through the bicone and the next B. Repeat seven more times to secure the pearl embellishment. Angle the needle to the center of the flower in the back of the pearl and push the needle to the back of the flower **(Fig . 18)**.

19 Align the bail to the back of the flower so that the loops are facing up and the flower seam is facing down or orientated as desired. Stitch the flower to the back of the bail ribbon with backstitches. I like to stitch into five areas of both the back of the flower and the bail backing in a cross formation. Tack down the center, Location 1, Location 2, Location 3, and Location 4 with backstitches. Use two repeats of backstitches in each location. Secure the thread and trim **(Fig. 19)**.

20 The bail slider is tacked and secured to the flower through the Cs from Step 11 with backstitches as performed in Step 18 for the front embellishment. Pick up a small amount of ribbon with the needle and pass back through the opposite end of the original C from front to back. Pass through the picot beads and the next C from Step 11. Repeat thirteen more times to secure the bail slider. Secure the thread and trim **(Fig. 20)**.

21 With your fingernails, fray the ribbon edge of the flower petals.

TIP

I like to fray about 2 mm off the edges in the same direction. Because the silk ribbon is bias, the fraying will occur at a slight angle. The fraying adds a new dimension and creates a livelier flower.

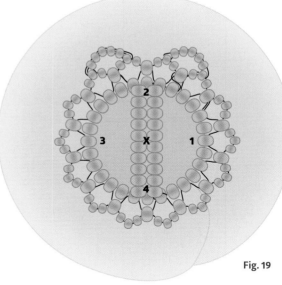

Fig. 19

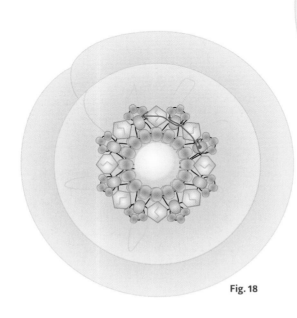

Fig. 18

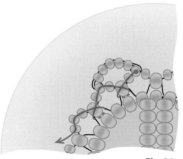

Fig. 20

{VARIATIONS}

↑ To create this version, use 1½" (3.8 cm) of cymbidium hand-dyed silk bias and 36" (91.5 cm) of purple haze metallic-edged hand-dyed silk tie.

↑ To create this version, use 1½" (3.8 cm) of lingerie hand-dyed silk bias and 36" (91.5 cm) of rose garden hand-dyed silk tie.

HANAMI

Hanami is Japanese for "beautiful flower." Two layers of three petals each are created with Glennis Dolce's (a.k.a. Shibori Girl) hand-dyed shibori silk satin bias ribbons. The pleating is removed to showcase the dyed pattern and variegated colors. The pattern and natural flow of the shibori beautifully mimic flower petal striations. The center component is embroidered with backstitches.

TECHNIQUES
unning stitch

ackstitch

rcular peyote stitch

itch-in-the-ditch mbellishment

callop edging

MATERIALS
75 g topaz rose-gold ster 11° Japanese ed beads (A)

35 g bronze 11° panese seed ads (B)

g gold-lined aqua ° Japanese seed ads (C)

75 g topaz rose-gold ° Japanese seed ads (D)

g bronze 15° panese seed ads (E)

g gold-lined aqua ° Japanese seed ads (F)

olcano 14mm rivoli nestone

vintage rose satin m Czech glass arls

23 cm) of dark k clover 4" (10 cm)

pleated hand-dyed bias ribbon

2" (5 cm) of chameleon ⅝" (1.5 cm) hand-dyed silk bias ribbon

36" (91.5 cm) of mango ½" (1.3 cm) hand-dyed silk tie

Cotton ball or scrap yarn

1 steel 12mm circular pin back

Double-sided 1" (2.5 cm) tape

Smoke 6 lb braided beading thread

TOOLS
Size 12 beading needles

Scissors

Fabric-marking pencil

Ruler

Iron

Rotary cutter and self-healing mat (optional)

SIZE
3¾" (9.5 cm) flower only

LEVEL
Intermediate

FORMING THE FLOWER

1 Using the silk setting of your iron, press the pleated ribbon to remove the pleats and reveal the beautiful dye pattern. Face the ribbon down and mark the ribbon into six 1½" (3.8 cm) sections. *(Note: The shiny side of the silk ribbon is the front side and the matte side is the back side.)* These will be the cutting guides. With a self-healing mat, rotary cutter, and the ruler as the cutting guide, cut the ribbon. Using a 24" (61 cm) length of thread, anchor the thread to the ribbon with a backstitch to secure. Start with the needle at the top of the ribbon ⅛" (3 cm) from the raw edge. Scoop up a little ribbon onto the needle, leaving about a ¼" (6 cm) thread tail. Repeat backstitching twice and gently tug on the thread. Proceed with a running stitch **(Fig. 1)**.

2 Pull the thread so the ribbon gathers to create the first flower petal. Secure the gather in place by repeating the backstitch as in Step 1 three times, then trim the thread. Repeat with the remaining five strips to create a total of six petals with the same working thread. Do not trim the thread on the last petal, as it will be used to connect the flower petals **(Fig. 2)**.

3 *Note: The flower has three petals on the bottom and three petals on top. The petals are stacked and stitched midway on each petal.* Overlap the first petal midway on top of the second petal. Stitch the petals together with three running backstitches **(Fig. 3)**. *(Note: A running backstitch is a backstitch that moves forward, in this case clockwise.)*

4 Overlap the third petal on top of the remaining half of the second petal. Stitch the petals together with three running backstitches **(Fig. 4)**.

5 Place the fourth petal midway to the back of the third petal. Stitch the petals together with three running backstitches **(Fig. 5)**.

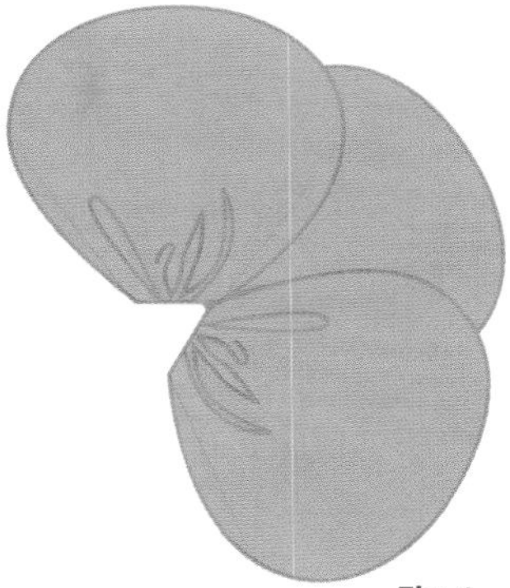

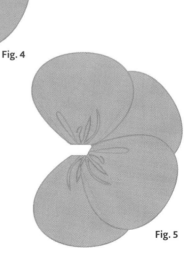

Fig. 4

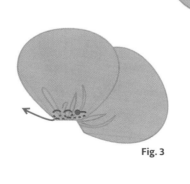

Fig. 3

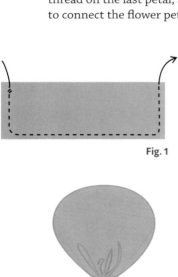

Fig. 2

Fig. 1

Fig. 5

Place the fifth petal on top of the remaining half of the fourth petal. Stitch [th]e petals together with three running [ba]ckstitches **(Fig. 6)**.

Place the remaining sixth petal [cen]tered on the back of the fifth and first [pe]tals. Stitch the sixth petal to the fifth [peta]l with three running backstitches. [Th]en stitch the sixth petal to the first [peta]l with another three running back-[sti]tches. Secure the thread and trim. Set [asi]de for assembly later **(Fig. 7)**.

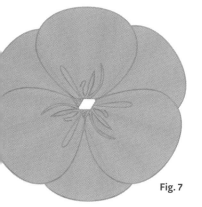

Fig. 6

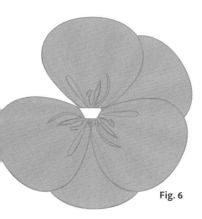

Fig. 7

TIP

Wear the pin as a pendant by stringing a silk tie or thin beaded rope through the loops created in Steps 20 and 21. You can add more beads to Step 19 and 20 when creating the bail loops to compensate for a thicker diameter necklace or rope.

ADDING THE RIVOLI EMBELLISHMENT

8 With a 60" (152.4 cm) length of thread, string 32A and join into a ring with a square knot, leaving an 8" (20.5 cm) tail. Pass through 1A away from the knot.

9 **ROUNDS 1–3:** Begin circular peyote stitch by stringing 1A, skipping 1A on the ring, and passing through the next A. Repeat fifteen more times. Step up through the first A added in this round.

ROUND 4: Work circular peyote stitch with 1A. Step up through the first A added in this round.

ROUND 5: Work circular peyote stitch with 1D. Step up through the first D added in this round.

ROUND 6: Work circular peyote stitch with 1E. Step up through the first E added in this round **(Fig. 8)**.

10 Insert the rivoli facedown into the bezel just created. The first round of circular peyote will then be facing up.

11 **ROUND 7:** Using the tail thread, work circular peyote stitch with 1D into the A from Round 1. Step up through the first D added in this round.

ROUND 8: Work circular peyote stitch with E. Step up through the first E added in this round. Secure the thread and trim **(Fig. 9)**.

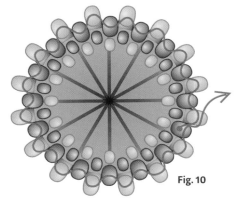

Fig. 8

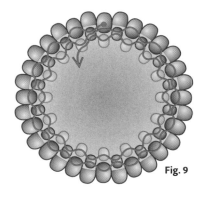

Fig. 9

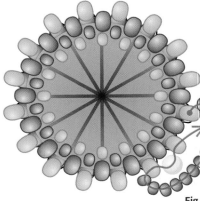

Fig.

Fig. 10

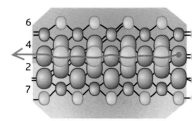

12 Flip the beadwork to the front. Weave thread to pass through 1A of Round 4 and stitch-in-the-ditch with 1B into each A of Round 4. Step up on the last stitch by weaving through the first B added in this step **(Fig. 10)**.

13 String 13D. Pass back through 1B two Bs away. String 1 pearl and pass through the next B. String 13E. Pass back through 1B two Bs away. String 1 pearl and pass through the next B. Repeat, alternating adding 13D and 13E scallops seven times. *Note: Be aware of the scallop loop fringe orientation on the last two connections to ensure same directional flow* **(Fig. 11)**.

14 Weave thread to pass through 1A of Round 3. Repeat stitch-in-the-ditch embellishment with 1B into every A of Round 3. Step up through the first B added in this round. Set aside for assembly later **(Fig. 12)**.

Fig. 12

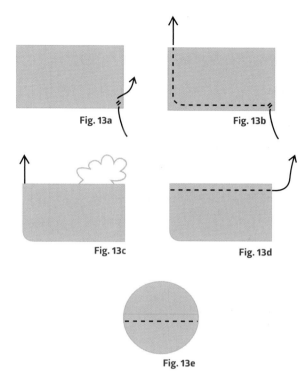

Fig. 13a **Fig. 13b**

Fig. 13c **Fig. 13d**

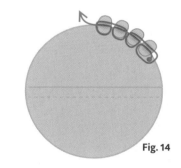

Fig. 13e

~NISHING THE BACK

Fold the ⅝" (1.5 cm) ribbon in half.
~te: *There is no front or back side to this*
~*bon*.) Using a 36" (91.5 cm) length of
~ead, anchor the thread to the ribbon
~ge, joining the folded ribbon with a
~kstitch. Start at the lower right cor-
~ of the ribbon edge ⅛" (3 mm) from
~ raw edge. Scoop up a little ribbon
~o the needle from both layers, leaving
~ut a ¼" (6 mm) thread tail **(Fig. 13a)**.
~peat backstitching twice and gently
~ on the thread. Proceed with a run-
~g stitch as shown in **Fig. 13b**. Secure
~ end and lock the stitch in place with
~eral backstitches. Flip the ribbon
~ket inside out. Fill the cavity with a
~all bit of cotton from the cotton ball
~use scrap yarn **(Fig. 13c)**. Proceed again
~h a running stitch **(Fig. 13d)**. Secure
~ thread and lock the stitches in place
~h several backstitches. Flatten the
~bon cushion with your fingers so the
~posed stitches are centered **(Fig. 13e)**.

🔟 Flip the ribbon cushion over. Weave
the needle to the edge. String 1C. Stitch
through the fabric one bead space away
and back up through to the front of the
C bead to create the first backstitch. Pass
back through the C. Repeat thirty-one
times for a total of thirty-two beads.
Step up by passing through the first C
(Fig. 14).

🔢 String 1C, skip 1C on the ring created
from Step 15, and pass through the
next C. Repeat fifteen times. Step up by
passing through the first C added in this
round **(Fig. 15)**.

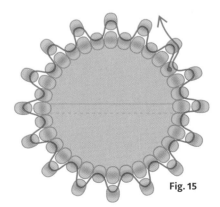

Fig. 14

Fig. 15

18 Apply the double-sided tape to the back of the pin-brooch finding. Trim around the edge. *Note: The double-sided tape helps the pin-brooch finding stay in place while securing it to the ribbon cushion during successive beading.* Adhere the finding to the back of the beadwork, taking care to ensure the pin connections are between two As from Step 16. String 3C. Skip 1C added in Step 16 and pass through the next C. Repeat around seven times. *Note: The beadwork will need to loop around the pin back in two locations. Since there will be eight picots, these two locations are three picots away from each other.* Reinforce the thread path to tighten the beadwork. Pass through to the second C of the first picot **(Fig. 16)**.

19 String 2F and pass through the second C (or center bead) of the next picot. Repeat around seven more times **(Fig. 17)**. Reinforce the thread path to further tighten the beadwork. Pass through the nearest C from Step 16 that is not connected to a picot.

20 String 5C, skip 1C, and pass through the next C not connected to a picot from Step 17. Repeat around seven times **(Fig. 18)**.

21 Pass through the third C (or center bead) of the picot two away from the pin back connection created in Step 19 (Location 1). String 9C and pass through the C between two picots created in Step 16 (Location 2). Pass back through all nine beads and into the opposite end of the original C of Location 1. Reinforce the thread path **(Fig. 19, blue thread)**.

22 Pass through the C at Location 3. Repeat Step 20 to create a second loop to Location 4 with 9C. Reinforce the thread path. Pass back through to the center bead of the picot at Location 3 **(Fig. 19, red thread)**.

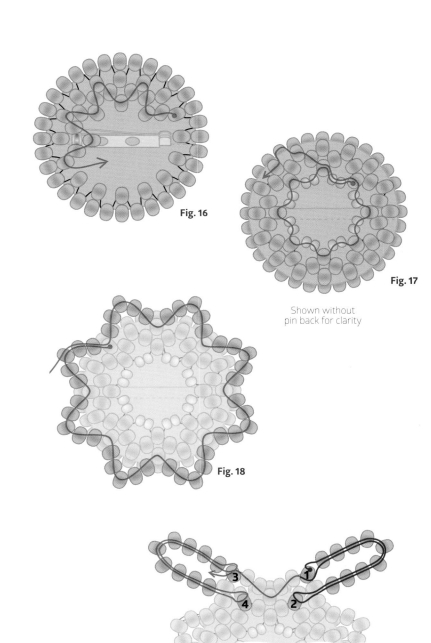

Fig. 16

Fig. 17

Shown without
pin back for clarity

Fig. 18

Fig. 19

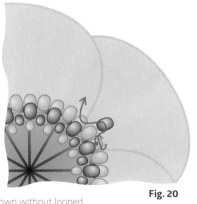

Shown without looped
embellishment for clarity

Fig. 20

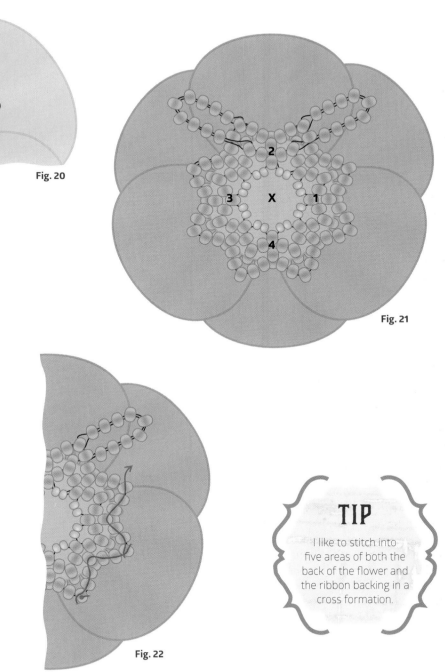

Fig. 21

Fig. 22

NNECTING IT TOGETHER

Place the rivoli embellishment at the
ter of the flower. The embellishment
l be tacked onto the ribbon with
kstitches through the B from Step
Pick up a small amount of ribbon
h the needle and pass back through
original B from front to back. String
and weave through the next B
. 20). Repeat fifteen times to secure
pearl embellishment. Angle the
dle to the center of the flower in the
k of the pearl and push the needle to
back of the flower.

Align the pin back to the back of
flower so that the loops are facing
Orient the flower from the front as
ired. Stitch the flower to the back
the pin back with backstitches. Tack
wn the center, Location 1, Location 2,
ation 3, and Location 4 with back-
ches. Use two repeats of backstitches
each location. Secure the thread and
n **(Fig. 21)**.

The pin-back beadwork is tacked and
ured to the flower with backstitches
ough the center Cs from Step 19.
k up a small amount of ribbon with
needle and weave back through the
posite end of the original C from front
back. Pass through the remaining
ads of this picot following the previous
read path to the next center bead of
subsequent picot from Step 19. Re-
t fifteen times to secure the pin back.
ure the thread and trim **(Fig. 22)**.

TIP

I like to stitch into
five areas of both the
back of the flower and
the ribbon backing in a
cross formation.

TECHNIQUES
Square stitch

Circular peyote stitch

Circular right-angle weave

Reverse picot

MATERIALS
9 g bronze-lined crystal 11° Japanese seed beads (A)

2.5 g bronze 11° Japanese seed beads (B)

6.5 g bronze-lined crystal 15° Japanese seed beads (C)

6.5 g bronze 15° Japanese seed beads (D)

104 golden shadow 3mm bicones

12 cream rose 6mm crystal pearls

130 cream rose 3mm crystal pearls

3 cream rose 11x8mm crystal drop pearls

13 golden shadow 6.5mm gold-plated 2-hole sliders

1 nickel-plated brass 3/0 sew-on snap set

Smoke 6 lb braided beading thread

TOOLS
Size 12 beading needles

Scissors

SIZE
19" (48.5 cm)

LEVEL
Advanced

CROWN JEWELS

NECKLACE

A mix of historical eras from Edwardian to Victorian (1400s to 1800s) influenced this necklace concept. Swarovski sew-on sliders sparkle like diamonds amidst pearls. The components and pearl drops are both captured with square-stitched bezels. This design represents the exuberance of the eras.

CREATING COMPONENT A

1 With a 36" (91.5 cm) length of thread, string the first hole of 1 slider and 2A. Pass through the second hole of the slider. String 2A and pass through the first hole of the slider and the first 2A added in this step. *Note: You may want to face the slider down with the back facing up for better visibility.* **(Fig. 1)**.

2 String 8A and pass through the second 2A. String another 8A and pass through the first 2A **(Fig. 2)**.

3 String 1A and square-stitch it to the A the thread is exiting. Pass through the next A around **(Fig. 3)**.

4 Repeat Step 3 nineteen times. On the last repeat, step up by passing through the first A added in Step 3.

Pass through all the added beads from this step, returning to the first A. Pull tight and the beads will pull up to bezel the slider **(Fig. 4)**. *(Note: There are two rounds of beads, one on top of the other, circling the slider each with twenty beads.)*

5 To begin circular peyote stitch, string 1B, skip an A on the bezel, and pass through the next A.

6 Repeat Step 5 nine more times. Step up through the first B added in Step 5 **(Fig. 5)**.

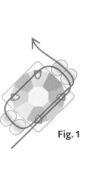

Fig. 1

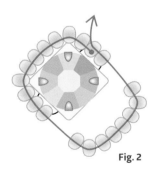

Fig. 2

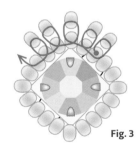

Fig. 3

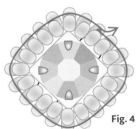

Fig. 4

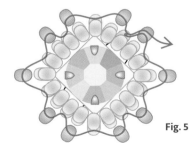

Fig. 5

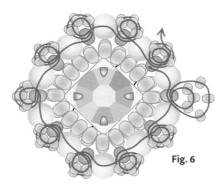

Fig. 6

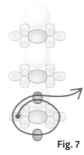

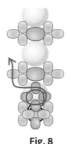

Fig. 7

Fig. 8

Fig. 9

Fig. 10

String one 3mm pearl and pass [thro]ugh the next B. String 3C. Pass [thro]ugh the opposite end of the B. Re-[pea]t stringing 3C and pass through the [opp]osite end of the B to create reverse [pico]ts **(Fig. 6)**. *Note: There are two reverse [pico]ts back to back.*

Repeat Step 7 nine times. Step [up] by weaving through the first 2C [of] the front picot (picot to the left) [(Fig. 6)**).

Turn the component sideways, with [the] back of the slider facing right and [the] crystal side facing left. String 1D and [pass] through the second C of the back [pico]t. String 1D and pass though the [seco]nd C of the front picot. Pass through [the] first D added in this step **(Fig. 7)**.

String 3D. Pass through the original [adj]oining D and the first two D added in [thi]s step. Pass through the second C of [the] next front picot **(Fig. 8)**.

11 *Note: Basically, we are attaching the two picots and finishing the edge of the component with right-angle weave. The component will have a rolled edge as you add right-angle-weave links.*

String 1D and pass through the second C on the rear picot, the adjoining D from the previous link, the second C on the front picot, and the D added in this step **(Fig. 9)**.

12 Repeat Steps 10–11 eight times.

13 To join, string 1D and pass through the adjoining D of the first link added in Step 9 **(Fig. 10)**.

14 String 1D and pass through the adjoining D of the ninth link. Reinforce through this connection by passing through the beads added in Step 13 and this step. Set aside for assembly later.

15 Flip the component so the slider is crystal side up. With the tail thread, pass through the top bezel beads to align around the slider. Pull tight as you pass through each side. Repeat twice. Secure the thread and trim.

16 Repeat Steps 1–15 twelve times to create a total of thirteen Component As. Three of these components will be combined with a drop element to create Component Bs.

TIP

Ease the beadwork toward the back as you stitch so the rolled edge does not collapse over the pearls.

CREATING COMPONENT B

17 With 1 Component A, pass through the second C of the rear picot at the corner of the component. To determine the corner of the component, use the prongs from the slider as the guide **(Fig. 11)**. *Note: Connections are always made through the second C of the rear picot.*

18 String 1 drop and 1A. Pass back through the drop and the second C of the rear picot **(Fig. 12)**.

19 String 15C and pass through the A at the bottom of the drop. String 15C. Pass through the second C of the rear picot and the first C added in this step **(Fig. 13)**.

20 String 1D and pass through the C circling the drop and the next C **(Fig. 14, green thread)**.

21 Repeat Step 20 fourteen times.

22 String 3D. Pass through the A at the bottom of the drop again and through the next C **(Fig. 14, blue thread)**.

23 Repeat Step 20 fifteen times. Pass through the second C of the rear picot. Add some thread tension and the bezel will form nicely around the drop. Secure the thread and trim **(Fig. 14, red thread)**.

24 Repeat Steps 17–23 twice to create a total of three Component Bs. Set aside for assembly later.

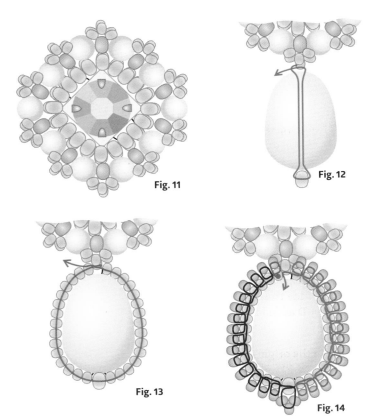

Fig. 11

Fig. 12

Fig. 13

Fig. 14

EATING COMPONENT C

With a 24" (61 cm) length of thread, ing one 6mm pearl and 7A. Pass ough the pearl again. Leave a 6" cm) tail. String 7A and pass through pearl again (**Fig. 15**).

Pass through the first set of 7A and ing 1A. Pass through the second set of and string 1A. Pass through the first gain, circling the pearl (**Fig. 16**).

String 1A and pass through the ginal A again, circling the pearl. Pass ough the next A (**Fig. 17**).

Repeat Step 27 fifteen times. On last repeat, pass through the A added he last repeat again, then through remaining 15As, returning back ough the first A. Pull tight and the ds will pull up to bezel the pearl . 18). *(Note: There are two rounds of ds, one on top of the other, circling the rl, each with sixteen beads.)*

Begin circular peyote stitch. String , skip 1A, and pass through the next A the lower bezel round (**Fig. 19**).

Repeat Step 29 seven times. Step up ough the first B added in Step 29.

String 1 bicone and pass through the ‹t B. String 3C and pass through the ginal B again. String another 3C and ss through the B once more to form : double reverse picots (**Fig. 20**).

Repeat Step 31 seven times. At the d of the last repeat, pass through the ond C of the front picot.

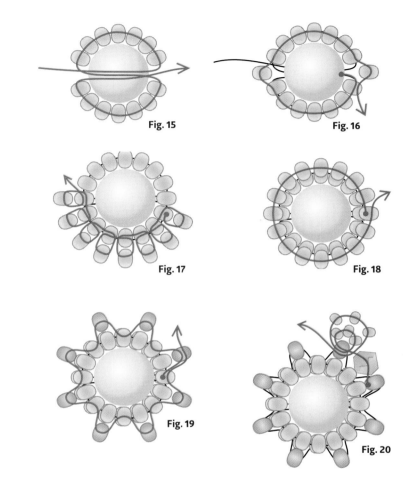

Fig. 15

Fig. 16

Fig. 17

Fig. 18

Fig. 19

Fig. 20

33 Turn the component sideways with the back facing right and the front facing left. String 1D and pass through the second C of the back picot. String 1D and pass though the second C of the front picot. Pass through the first D added in this step (**Fig. 21**).

34 String 3D. Pass through the original adjoining D again and the first 2D added in this step. Pass through the second C of the next front picot (**Fig. 22**).

35 String 1D. Pass through the second C on the rear picot, the adjoining D from the previous link, the second C on the front picot, and the D added in this step **(Fig. 23)**.

36 *Note: As with Component A, Component C will have a rolled edge as you add right-angle-weave links. Ease the beadwork toward the back as you stitch so that the rolled edge does not collapse over the bicones. Repeat Steps 34–35 six times.*

37 To join, string 1D. Pass through the adjoining D of the first link added in Step 34 **(Fig. 24)**.

38 String 1D, then pass through the adjoining D of the seventh link. Reinforce through this connection by passing through the beads added in Step 37 and this step again. Set aside for assembly later.

39 Flip the component so that the front is facing up. With the tail thread, pass through the top bezel beads to align around the pearl, pulling tight. Repeat twice. Secure the thread and trim.

40 Repeat Steps 25–39 ten times to create a total of eleven Component Cs.

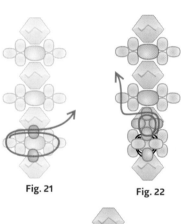

Fig. 21   **Fig. 22**

Fig. 23   **Fig. 24**

CREATING THE SNAP CLOSURE

41 Repeat Steps 25–32 from Component C. Start with a 36" (91.5 cm) length of thread and leave a 12" (30.5 cm) tail for sewing the snap.

42 Use the tail thread and pass through an A on the bottom bezel. Use the male portion of the snap with a flat back. *Note: There are sixteen beads circling the bottom of the pearl. There are four openings on the snap. Each connection is four beads away from each other.*

43 String the thread through one of the openings on the snap from the bottom up. Pass through the A again. Repeat this connection twice more to secure the snap onto the beadwork. Pass through the next 4A around **(Fig. 25)**.

44 Repeat Step 43 three times. Secure the tail thread and trim.

45 *Note: The snap will be easier to add to the beadwork before finishing the edges with right-angle weave. Repeat Steps 33–39 from Component C.*

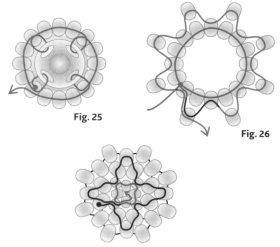

Fig. 25

Fig. 26

Fig. 27

46 Since the tail thread was used to sew on the snap, use the working thread to align the A beads on the top bezel. Pass through the beadwork following the previous thread path to an A on the top bezel. Pass through the top bezel beads to align around the pearl, pulling tight. Repeat twice. Secure the thread and trim.

47 *Note: The other side of the beaded snap is designed differently because the female snap has a domed back.* With a 36" (91.5 cm) length of thread, string 16A and join into a ring with a square knot, leaving a 12" (30.5 cm) tail. Pass through 1A away from the knot **(Fig. 26, green thread)**.

48 String 1A, skip 1A on the ring, and pass through the next A **(Fig. 26, blue thread)**.

49 Repeat Step 48 seven times. Step up through the first A added in Step 48 **(Fig 26, red thread)**.

50 Repeat Steps 29–32 from Component C.

51 Repeat Steps 42–44 to add the female snap to the beadwork with the tail thread.

52 To reduce the opening on the back of the snap, pass through the beadwork following the previous thread path to an A on the first peyote round from Step 48.

53 String 1C, then pass through the next A on the first peyote round, through the adjoining A from the second round, and back up to the following A on the first round **(Fig. 27, blue thread)**.

54 Repeat Step 53 three times. Step up through the first C added in Step 53.

55 String 1C and pass through the C added in Step 54.

56 Repeat Step 55 three times. Circle around the beadwork to tighten **(Fig. 27, red thread)**. Secure the tail thread and trim.

57 Repeat Steps 33–39 from Component C.

58 Repeat Step 46.

CONNECTING THE COMPONENTS

59 *Note: Refer to* **Fig. 28.** *Connection 1 and 2 connects a Component B with a Component C. Again, all connections are made through the second C on the rear picot embellishment. Attachments are made viewing from the back of beadwork. The connection mimics fine chain. If more spacing is desired between components, this is where extra Ds can be added.* Flip the beadwork to the back so the rear picot beads can be easily reached and seen. From Component C, pass through the second C of a rear picot. This will be Connection 1.

60 String 3D, then pass through the second C of a rear picot on Component B, four picots away from its drop connection. Pass back through the 3D and the original second C of the rear picot from Component C. Reinforce the connection and pass back through the C on Component B **(Fig. 29, green thread).**

61 To reach Connection 2 on Component C, follow the right-angle-weave thread path and pass through to the second C of the rear picot one picot away from Connection 1 **(Fig. 29, blue thread).**

62 String 3D, then pass through the second C of the rear picot two picots away from Connection 1. Pass back through the 3D and the original C on Component C again. Reinforce the connection and pass back through the C on Component B **(Fig. 29, red thread).**

63 To reach Connection 3 on Component C, follow the right-angle-weave thread path and pass through the second C of the rear picot two picots away from Connection 2.

64 String 3D, then pass through the second C of the rear picot one picot away from the drop connection on a second Component B. Pass back through the 3D and the original second C of the rear picot from Component C. Reinforce the

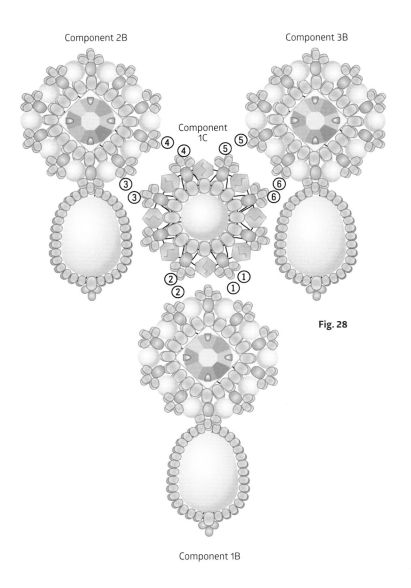

Component 2B

Component 3B

Component 1C

Fig. 28

Component 1B

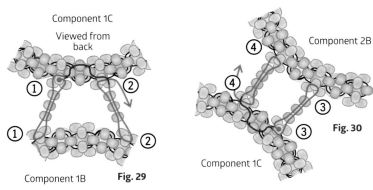

Component 1C
Viewed from back

Component 1B   Fig. 29

Component 2B

Component 1C   Fig. 30

nection and pass back through the
n the second Component B **(Fig. 30,**
n thread).

To reach Connection 4 on Compo-
t C, follow the right-angle-weave
ead path and pass through the second
f the rear picot one picot away from
nection 3 **(Fig. 30, blue thread)**.

String 4D, then pass through the
nd C of the rear picot one picot away
n Connection 3. Pass back through
4D and the opposite end of the orig-
second C of the rear picot from Com-
ent C. Reinforce the connection and
s back through the C on the second
nponent B **(Fig. 30, red thread)**.

To reach Connection 5 on Compo-
t C, following the right-angle-weave
ead path, pass through the second
f the rear picot one picot away from
nection 4.

String 4D. Pass through the second C
he rear picot, two picots away from
drop connection on the third Com-
ent B. Pass back through the 4D and
opposite end of the original second
f the rear picot from Component C.
nforce the connection and pass back
ough the C on the third Component B
31, green thread).

To reach Connection 6 on Compo-
t C following the right-angle-weave
ead path, pass through the second
f the rear picot one picot away from
nection 5 **(Fig. 31, blue thread)**.

String 3D, then pass through the
nd C of the rear picot one picot
y from the drop connection on the
d Component B. Pass back through
3D and the opposite end of the
inal second C of the rear picot from
nponent C. Reinforce the connec-
. Secure the thread and trim **(Fig. 31,**
thread).

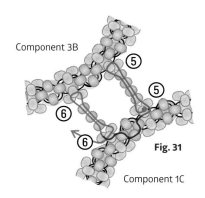

Component 3B

⑤
⑤
⑥
⑥

Fig. 31

Component 1C

71 All remaining connections will be
made with 3D. Connect a Component C to
the third Component B as shown in **Fig. 32**
through the respective C of the rear picot
at Connection 7 and 8. For Connection 7,
pass through the C of the rear picot three
picots away from the drop connection on
the third Component B. Follow the right-
angle-weave thread path as in previous
steps when changing weaving direction
between connections. Secure the thread
and trim.

72 Connect the Component C from Step
71 to a Component A as shown in **Fig. 33**
through the respective C of the rear picot
at Connection 9 and 10. For Connection
9, pass through the C of the rear picot
three picots away from Connection 7.
*Note: Ensure when attaching any Compo-
nent As that the connection is made one
picot away from the corner prong of the
slider.* Secure the thread and trim.

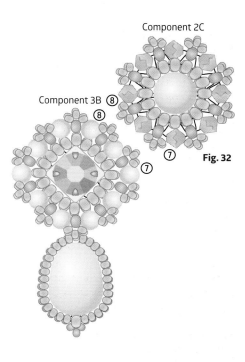

Component 2C

Component 3B ⑧
⑧
⑦
⑦

Fig. 32

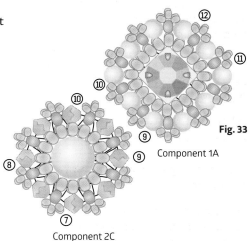

⑫
⑪
⑩
⑩
⑨
⑨
⑧
⑦

Fig. 33

Component 1A

Component 2C

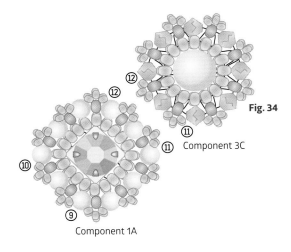

Fig. 34

Component 3C

Component 1A

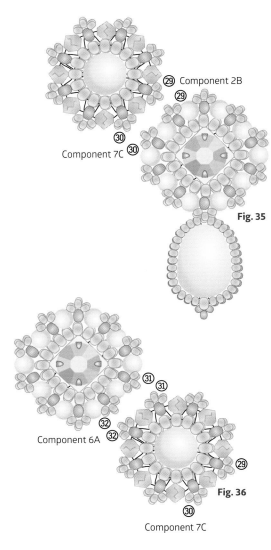

Component 2B

Component 7C

Fig. 35

Component 6A

Fig. 36

Component 7C

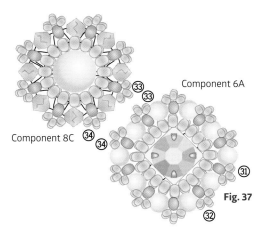

Component 6A

Component 8C

Fig. 37

73 Connect the Component A from Step 72 to a Component C as shown in **Fig. 34** through the respective C of the rear picot at Connection 11 and 12. For Connection 11, pass through the C of the rear picot four picots away from Connection 9. Secure the thread and trim.

74 Repeat Steps 72–73 three times, alternating between Component A and Component C. Secure the thread and trim after each component is connected.

75 Repeat Step 72 with the last Component A on this side of the necklace. Secure the thread and trim.

76 Repeat Step 73 to attach the bottom snap with the snap facing up. Secure the thread and trim.

77 Connect a Component C to the second Component B as shown in **Fig. 35** through the respective C of the rear picot at Connection 29 and 30. For Connection 30, pass through the C of the rear picot three picots away from the drop connection on the second Component B. Secure the thread and trim.

Connect the Component C from Step
to a Component A as shown in **Fig. 36**
ough the respective C of the rear picot
Connection 31 and 32. For Connection
ensure that the connection is two
ots away from the corner prong of the
der and pass through the C of the rear
ot three picots away from Connection
Secure the thread and trim.

Connect the Component A from Step
to a Component C as shown in **Fig. 37**
ough the respective C of the rear picot
Connection 33 and 34. For Connection
pass through the C of the rear picot
r picots away from Connection 32.
ure the thread and trim.

Repeat Steps 78–79 three times,
ernating between Component A and
mponent C. Secure the thread and
n after each component is connected.

Repeat Step 78 with the last Compo-
t A. Secure the thread and trim.

Repeat Step 79 to attach the top snap
h the pearl faceup. Secure the thread
d trim.

VARIATION

To create this variation,
use 3mm, 6mm, and 11x8mm
gray pearls, hematite bicones,
jet gold-plated sliders, a black
3/0 sew-on snap set, and
hematite seed beads for A and
C. Use the same seed beads
as the main project colorway
for B and D.

ECHNIQUES

ibular peyote stitch

ght-angle weave

erringbone stitch

quare stitch

etting

itch-in-the-ditch
nbellishment

cot

pping

ATERIALS

g purple hematite
° Japanese seed
ads (A)

bronze 11°
panese seed
ads (B)

blue gold luster
° Japanese seed
ads (C)

g matte gray blue
ld iris 11° Japanese
ed beads (D)

matte bronze
vine iris 11°
panese seed
ads (E)

purple hematite
° Japanese seed
ads (F)

bronze 15°
panese seed
ads (G)

blue gold luster
° Japanese seed
ads (H)

matte steel green
d iris 11° Japanese
d beads (J)

1.5 g light
amethyst AB 15°
Japanese seed
beads (K)

3 light vitrail 14mm
rivoli rhinestones

3 light sapphire
glacier 14mm rivoli
rhinestones

160 gold 3mm
vintage crystal pearls

10 gold 4mm vintage
crystal pearls

32 gold 2mm
Czech glass pearls

70 blue turquoise
Picasso 3x6mm
2-hole cylinder
beads (L)

38 blue turquoise
Picasso 3mm fire-
polished glass rounds

4 antiqued brass
12x5mm barrel
clasps

Smoke 6 lb braided
beading thread

TOOLS

Size 12 beading
needles

No-Tangle bobbin

Scissors

SIZE
15¾" (40 cm)

LEVEL
Advanced

ENCANTO
NECKLACE

The epitome of this book's theme is the Encanto necklace. The metamorphosis takes place when you reconfigure the necklace by unscrewing and reattaching the hidden barrel clasps. The medallions are reversible, and the centerpiece focals are bezeled rivolis with a floral motif. The details are further enhanced in the unique necklace rope created with Rullas, two-hole cylinder beads. I like designing jewelry that is both functional and beautiful with the versatility of reversibility.

BEZELING THE RIVOLI CENTERS

1 With a 60" (152.4 cm) length of thread, string 20F and join into a ring with a square knot, leaving a 6" (15 cm) tail. Pass through 1F away from the knot.

2 ROUNDS 1–3: String 1F, skip 1F on the ring, and pass through the next F. Repeat around nine times. Step up through the first F added in this round **(Fig. 1)**.

3 ROUND 4: String 2F into each of the Fs added in Round 3. Step up through the first 2F added in this round **(Fig. 2)**.

4 ROUND 5: String 1A into each of the paired Fs added in Step 3. Treat the 2F as a single unit. Step up through the first A added in this round **(Fig. 3)**.

5 ROUND 6: String 2A into each of the As from Step 4. Step up through the first paired As added in this round **(Fig. 4)**.

6 ROUND 7: String 3F into each set of paired As added in Step 5. Treat the 2A as a single unit. Step up through the first 2F added in this round **(Fig. 5)**.

7 ROUND 8: String 3F into the second A (or center bead) of each of the picots added in Step 6. Before joining the last two picots, insert the light vitrail rivoli faceup in the bezel just created. Step up through the first 3F added in this round **(Fig. 6)**.

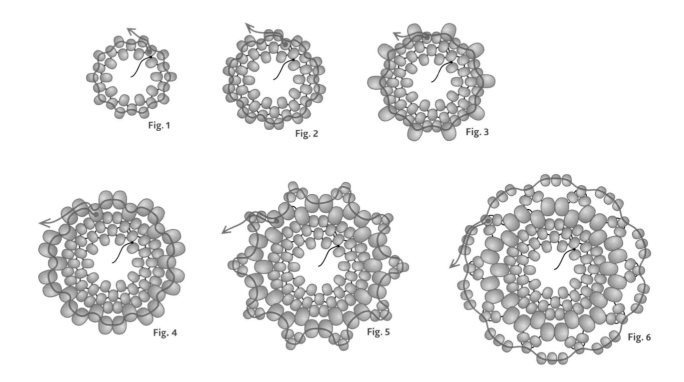

Fig. 1

Fig. 2

Fig. 3

Fig. 4

Fig. 5

Fig. 6

8 **ROUND 9:** String 1B through each of the 3Fs from Step 7. Treat each of the 3F as a single unit. Step up through the first B added in this round **(Fig. 7)**.

9 **ROUND 10:** String 2G into each of the Bs from Step 8. Step up through the first G added in this round **(Fig. 8)**.

10 To create the floral motif around the front of the rivoli, string 3G and pass through the second G of the next paired Gs from Step 9. Pass through the subsequent B and the following G. Repeat around four times. Pass down to Round 6 through a pair of Bs **(Fig. 9)**.

11 Repeat Step 6 by stringing 3G into each set of paired As of Round 6. Treat the 2A as a single unit. Step up through the first 3G added and the subsequent A. Secure the tail thread and trim. Set aside the working thread for assembly later **(Fig. 10)**.

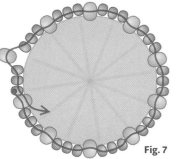

Fig. 7

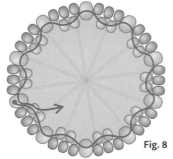

Fig. 8

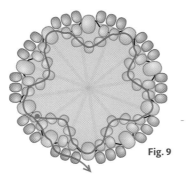

Fig. 9

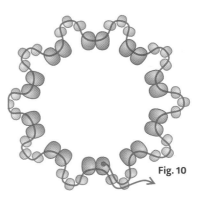

Fig. 10

12 Repeat Steps 1–11 to create two more Rivoli 1s. Repeat Steps 1–10 to create three Rivoli 2s, switching to C and H with the light sapphire glacier rivolis.

CONNNECTING THE RIVOLIS

13 Match up Rivoli 1 and Rivoli 2 so their backs touch. Ensure the flower petals of each rivoli bezel line up. With the thread from Rivoli 1, string 1B and zip it to Rivoli 2 by weaving through the opposing paired Cs in a zigzag motion. Repeat with 1B, weaving from Rivoli 2 to Rivoli 1 **(Fig. 11)**.

14 Repeat Step 13 four times to zip the rivolis together. Using the thread from Rivoli 2, zip to secure the joint. Secure both threads and trim. Repeat joining the remaining rivolis for two additional joined units **(Fig. 12)**.

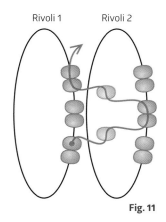

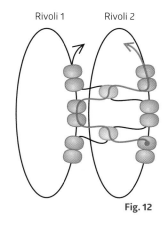

Rivoli 1 Rivoli 2   Rivoli 1 Rivoli 2

Fig. 11   **Fig. 12**

CREATING THE LARGEST REVERSIBLE FOCAL

15 With a 60" (152.4 cm) length of thread, add new thread through the Bs of the peyote-joined round from the last section between Rivoli 1 and Rivoli 2. Stitch-in-the-ditch by stringing 2C and passing through the next B. Repeat around nine times. Step up through the first C added in this step **(Fig. 13)**.

16 String 5C and pass down the second C from Step 15 **(Fig. 14, blue thread)**. String a fire-polished round and 3G. Pass back through the fire-polished round and the first C of the next pair of Cs from Step 15 **(Fig. 14, red thread)**. Repeat this entire step nine times. Step up to the first C added in this step.

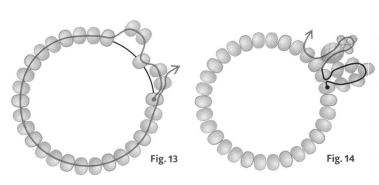

Fig. 13   Fig. 14

Cut away to show bronze
bead between rivolis

Reinforce the beadwork to stiffen the ~~al~~ by passing down the fifth C of the ~~t~~ 5-bead unit from Step 16 and the ~~elow~~ the fire-polished round. Pass ~~through~~ to the first C of the second ~~ead~~ unit. Repeat around to reinforce ~~beadwork~~ **(Fig. 15, blue thread)**. Step up ~~the~~ third C (or center bead) of the first ~~ead~~ unit **(Fig. 15, red thread)**.

String 3J and pass through the ~~ond~~ G of the picot above the fire-~~ished~~ round added in Step 16 **(Fig. 16, ~~e~~ thread)**. String 3J and pass through ~~third~~ C of the second 5-bead unit ~~g. 16, red thread)~~. Repeat this entire step ~~e~~ times. Step up through the third C ~~the~~ first 5-bead unit.

String one 4mm pearl and 1G. Pass ~~ck~~ through the pearl and through the ~~gain~~. Pass through the 3G, the center ~~he~~ 3J, and the second B (or center ~~d)~~ **(Fig. 17)**. Repeat around nine times ~~stiffen~~ the beadwork and add the ~~naining~~ 4mm pearls. Step up through ~~first~~ pearl and G added in this step.

String 5J and pass through the center ~~String~~ another 5J and pass through ~~G~~ above the pearl **(Fig. 18)**. Repeat ~~s~~ entire step nine times. Step up to ~~second~~ J added in this step.

Use square stitch to embellish the ~~ads~~ added in Step 20. String 1K and ~~ss~~ through the J again and through ~~next~~ J. Repeat three times, with the ~~t~~ repeat weaving through the G above ~~pearl~~ **(Fig. 19)**.

String 3G. Pass through the G above ~~pearl~~ and through the next J. Repeat ~~are~~ stitch with 1K four times as in ~~p~~ 21. Pass through the last J. String ~~and~~ pass through the first 2J of the ~~xt~~ sequence **(Fig. 20)**.

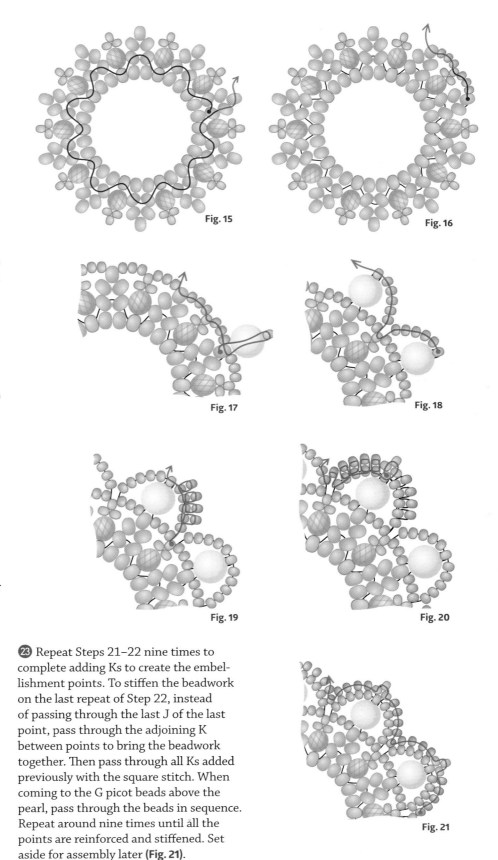

Fig. 15

Fig. 16

Fig. 17

Fig. 18

Fig. 19

Fig. 20

23 Repeat Steps 21–22 nine times to complete adding Ks to create the embellishment points. To stiffen the beadwork on the last repeat of Step 22, instead of passing through the last J of the last point, pass through the adjoining K between points to bring the beadwork together. Then pass through all Ks added previously with the square stitch. When coming to the G picot beads above the pearl, pass through the beads in sequence. Repeat around nine times until all the points are reinforced and stiffened. Set aside for assembly later **(Fig. 21)**.

Fig. 21

CREATING THE SECONDARY REVERSIBLE FOCALS

24 *Note: The secondary focals are created similarly as the large focal, but several steps have different bead counts to create a smaller complementary component.* Repeat Step 15. Repeat Step 16 with the following modifications: String 3C and pass through the second C from Step 15. String a fire-polished round and 1G. Pass back through the fire-polished round and through the first C of the next paired Cs from Step 15. Repeat this entire step nine times. Step up through the second C added in this step **(Fig. 22)**.

25 String 3J and pass through the G above the fire-polished round from Step 24. String 3J and pass through the second C (or center bead) from Step 24. Repeat this entire step nine times. Step up to the second C added in this step **(Fig. 23)**.

26 String one 3mm pearl and 1G. Pass back through the pearl and through the C again. Pass through the 3J, the G, the 3J, and the subsequent center B **(Fig. 24)**. Repeat around nine times to stiffen the beadwork and to add the 3mm pearls. Step up through the first pearl and the G added in this step.

27 String 4J and pass through the G above the fire-polished round. String another 4J and pass through the G above the pearl **(Fig. 25)**. Repeat this entire step nine times. Step up to the second J added in Step 24.

28 Use square stitch to embellish the beads added in Step 27. String 1K. Pass through the J and through the next J. Repeat twice, with the last repeat passing through the G above the pearl **(Fig. 26)**.

29 String 3G. Pass through the G above the pearl and through the next J. Use square stitch with Ks three times as in Step 28. Pass through the last J. String 1K. Pass through the first 2J of the next sequence **(Fig. 27)**.

30 Repeat Steps 28–29 nine times to complete adding Ks to create the embellishment points. To stiffen the beadwork on the last repeat of Step 29, pass through the adjoining K between points to bring the beadwork together instead of weaving through the last J of the last point. Pass through all Ks added previously with square stitch. When coming to the G picot beads above the pearl, pass through the beads in sequence **(Fig. 28)**. Repeat around nine times until all the points are reinforced and stiffened. Set aside for assembly later. Repeat Steps 24–30 for another secondary focal.

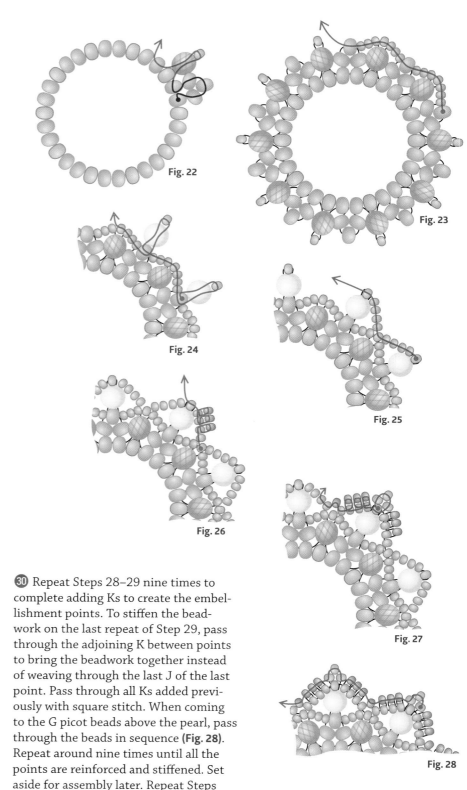

Fig. 22

Fig. 23

Fig. 24

Fig. 25

Fig. 26

Fig. 27

Fig. 28

CREATING THE NECKLACE BAND

With a 120" (304.8 cm) length of thread, wrap half of the thread onto a No-Tangle bobbin. String 1E and 1D. Treat these two beads as one unit to create a stop bead by passing through both beads again **(Fig. 29)**.

String 1L and 1D. Repeat sixty-eight times. String 1L, 1D, and 1E. There should be a total of 70L strung with 1D between each L. Pass through the second hole of the last L. String 1E to connect the second hole of the remaining Ls sixty-nine times **(Fig. 30)**.

Pass through the last L. Unroll the thread from the No-Tangle bobbin and remove the stop bead pair but keep the D and E strung. Roll the working thread onto the No-Tangle bobbin. Add a needle to the tail thread and pass back through the last L in the opposite direction of the working thread. Pass through the joining E **(Fig. 31)**.

TIP
When new thread is required, add through the center of the necklace band between the Ls and the respective D or E to avoid tension issues.

34 Flip the beadwork so that the circular side of the cylinder-shaped L has the Es facing up for better beading visibility. *String 3E and pass through the opposite end of the E between two Ls. Repeat with another 3E. Pass through the next L and into the subsequent E between two Ls. Repeat from * sixty-eight times. Pass through the last L **(Fig. 32)**.

35 Pass through the edge E and D to the opposite L side. Flip the beadwork to the D side for better visibility. Pass through the L and the following D. As in Step 34, string 3D and pass through the opposite end of the D between two Ls. Repeat with another 3D. Pass through the next L and through the subsequent D between two Ls. Repeat this entire step sixty-eight times. Pass through the last L **(Fig. 33)**.

Fig. 29

Fig. 30

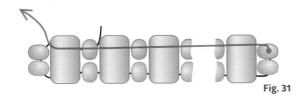

Fig. 31

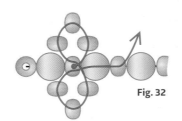

Fig. 32

36 Flatten the two picots added on both sides with your fingers. The Ds and Es will be on opposite sides with their same colored beads on the same axis **(Fig. 34)**.

37 The sides will be zipped with right-angle weave. Pass through the edge D and E. String 2G, one 3mm pearl, and 2G. Pass back through the edge D and E, the first 2G, and the pearl **(Fig. 35)**.

38 String 1G, then pass through the second E (or center bead) of its first picot (bottom). String 1G, then pass through the original pearl, the G, the second D (or center bead) of its first picot (top), the G, and the pearl just added in this step **(Fig. 36)**.

39 Repeat Step 38. *Note: The beading direction will switch to the opposite direction.* String 1G, then pass through the second E of its next picot. String 1G, one 3mm pearl, and 1G. Pass through the complementary second D of its next picot. String 1G, then pass through the original pearl, the G, the center E, the G, and the pearl just added in this step **(Fig. 37)**.

40 Repeat Steps 38–39 thirty-three times.

41 Repeat Step 37.

42 String 2G through the edge E and D. String 2G, then pass through the last pearl, the first 2G, and both the center D and the center E of the last picot. Flip the beadwork over and repeat Steps 37–42 to zip up the other edge of the collar. Secure the threads through the end D and E for assembly later **(Fig. 38)**.

Fig. 33

Fig. 34

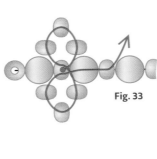

Fig. 35

Fig. 36

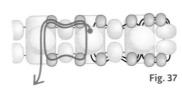

Fig. 37

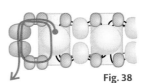

Fig. 38

Fig. 39

Fig. 40

ADED BARREL- ASP CONNECTORS

With an 18" (45.5 cm) length of
ead, string 1B, one fire-polished
nd, and 1B. Pass through the male
tion of the barrel clasp, leaving a 6"
cm) tail. String 1G, then pass back
ough the barrel clasp, the B, the
-polished round, and the B **(Fig. 39)**.

String 8G, then pass back through
B, the fire-polished round, the B, and
barrel clasp. String another G, then
s back through the barrel clasp, the
he fire-polished round, the B, and the
t G added in this step **(Fig. 40)**.

Square-stitch the loop to create a
re secure connection. String 1G, then
s back through the opposite end
he G on the loop and through the
t subsequent G on the loop. Repeat
en times, with the last repeat passing
ough the B and the fire-polished
nd. Pass under the thread of a previ-
thread pass and tie a half-hitch knot
41).

Pass back through the fire-polished
nd, the B, and through all the Gs
led in Step 45 to align stitches. Pass
k through the B, the fire-polished
nd, and the B. Again, pass under the
ead from a previous thread pass and
a half-hitch knot. Pass back through

the B and repeat tying a half-hitch
knot between the fire-polished round.
Secure both working and tail threads
through the loop and trim **(Fig. 42)**.

47 With a 24" (61 cm) length of
thread, string 2K and 2G. Repeat
stringing in this sequence three times
to have four repeats. Join into a ring
with a square knot, leaving a 12"
(30.5 cm) tail. Pass through 1K away
from the knot **(Fig. 43)**.

48 ROUNDS 1–3: To create a peyote
tube that will slide onto the barrel
clasp, flip the ring vertically for beading visibility. String 1G, skip 1K onto
the ring, and pass through the 1G.
String 1K, skip 1G on the ring, and
pass through the 1K. Repeat around,
alternating between a G and a K three
times. Step up through the first G
added in this round **(Fig. 44)**. *Note: By
always stringing the opposite bead from
which your thread is exiting, you create
the spiral effect.*

Fig. 41

Fig. 42

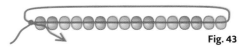

Fig. 43

TIP
To open the barrel clasps, spread the beadwork from the center gently.
With light tension, press down on the beadwork with your fingers to
grip and unscrew. To close the barrel clasps, screw on the clasp and align
the spirals by pushing the beadwork to the center. The beadwork on the
barrel clasp actually spins easily for these maneuvers.

49 ROUNDS 4–6: Slide the tube onto the male end of the barrel clasp from Step 46. Repeat the peyote spiral by alternating the G and K for three rounds. Secure the working thread and trim **(Fig. 45)**.

50 With the tail thread, pass through to the G on Round 1. String 5G, then pass back through the next G on Round 1. Repeat three times. Step up to the third G (or center bead) of the first 5-bead picot **(Fig. 46)**.

51 String one 2mm pearl. Pass back through the third G of the subsequent 5-bead picot. Repeat three times to add a total of four 2mm pearls. Tighten the beadwork by passing through all beads twice. Secure the thread and trim **(Fig. 47)**.

52 Repeat Steps 43–51 for the female portion of the barrel clasp. Create three more beaded barrel clasps for a total of four clasps. Leave the male and female portions unattached for assembly.

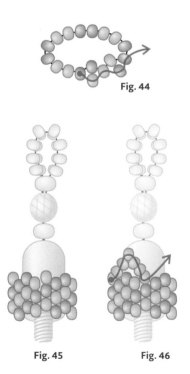

Fig. 44

Fig. 45   Fig. 46

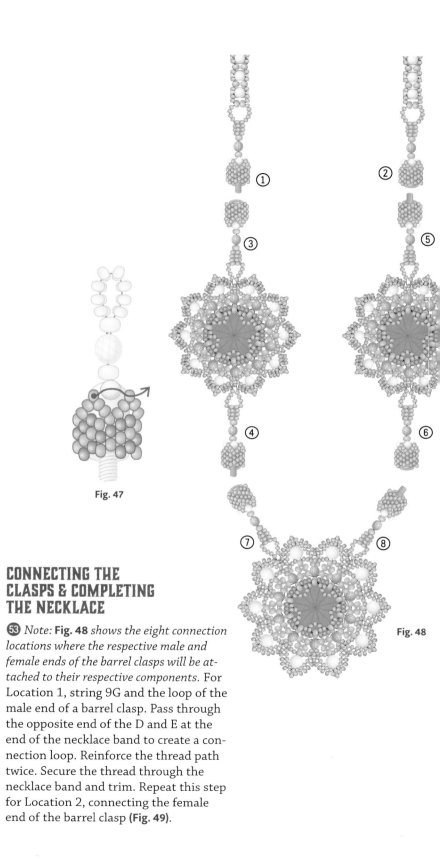

Fig. 47

CONNECTING THE CLASPS & COMPLETING THE NECKLACE

53 *Note:* **Fig. 48** *shows the eight connection locations where the respective male and female ends of the barrel clasps will be attached to their respective components.* For Location 1, string 9G and the loop of the male end of a barrel clasp. Pass through the opposite end of the D and E at the end of the necklace band to create a connection loop. Reinforce the thread path twice. Secure the thread through the necklace band and trim. Repeat this step for Location 2, connecting the female end of the barrel clasp **(Fig. 49)**.

Fig. 48

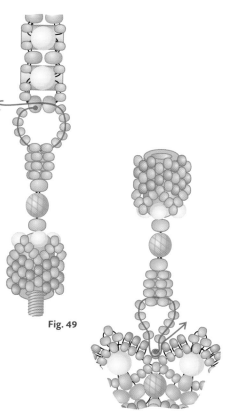

Fig. 49

Fig. 50

Fig. 51

54 With one secondary focal, pass through the K as shown between two points on **Fig. 48**. *Note: It is important to align the flower bezel accent.* For Location 3, string 9G and the loop of the female end of a barrel clasp. Pass through the opposite end of the K to create a connection loop **(Fig. 50)**. Reinforce the thread path twice. Pass through five points away to the complementary opposite K on **Fig. 48** noted as Location 4.

55 String 9G and the loop of the male end of a barrel clasp. Pass through the opposite end of the K to create a connec-tion loop. Reinforce through the thread path twice. Secure the thread and trim **(Fig. 51)**.

56 Repeat Steps 54–55 for Locations 5 and 6 **(Figs. 48, 50, and 51)**. *Note: The barrel clasps are attached in reverse, with Location 5 connected to the male end of a barrel clasp and Location 6 connected to the female end of a barrel clasp.*

57 Repeat Steps 54–55 for Locations 7 and 8 **(Figs. 48, 50, and 51)**. *Note: Location 7 is connected to the female end of a barrel clasp. Location 8 is located two points clockwise from Location 7 and is connected to the male end of a barrel clasp.*

TIP

The necklace is both interchangeable and reversible. It can be worn with one secondary focal connected, two secondary focals connected consecutively, or just with the center larger focal. The other option is to connect all three focals as shown on page 130. The flexibility of this design is that you can create other components that can be switched out as desired.

COLOR & INSPIRATION

COLOR & TEXTURE

I've had a love affair with color and texture for as long as I can remember, even before I became a beadweaver, glass beadmaker, and jewelry designer. I grew up around beautiful textiles with both parents deeply immersed in the fashion industry. As a child, I used to touch the fabrics at my parents' shop to feel the texture, and I looked at color all day. To this day, I still love touching fabrics and look to fashion as a color guide.

I'm often asked how I select the colors for my designs. Am I lucky enough to have a personal color goddess that follows me around when I buy beads or design? After all, many beaders are more comfortable in following a pattern in a magazine or a book where all the colors and materials have been itemized. But when it comes to selecting their own colors, the thought of leaving their comfort zones is almost like pulling teeth. I think that we sometimes make things more difficult than they really are. I always want to challenge my fellow beaders to select their own colorways when attempting one of my patterns.

Although I think a cursory knowledge of color concepts is important, I personally have never taken a color theory course or studied the subject in depth. If you are confused with analogous, tetradic, triadic, and split complementary colors, then let me show you an easier way to design that's FUN in the process!

There are so many books for every artistic medium that cover the gamut of color theories; they all suggest you buy a color wheel to help along the way. I have seen beaders who use a color wheel, and their color selections do not always blend well or look harmonious. So owning a color wheel and knowing how it works is not totally fail-safe. Most color choices are dependent on our intuition and what is pleasing to our individual eyes. It may be somewhat dependent on our wardrobe or a mood we wish to convey. Trust yourself! You know more about color than you think.

So what's the secret to choosing the right colors that blend well for excellent visual appeal and texture? Here are a dozen tricks and ideas that I use in my work that I hope will help you:

Build your bead stash.

When shopping for beads, I don't always have a project in mind. I pick beads for their shape and color first, to build my bead stash. The more beads you have in your stash, the more variety of designs you can execute later. If budget is on your mind, I suggest focusing on special stones, shapes, and colors that are harder to find because the more common components will be easily accessible later. A design will surface on its own when the right time approaches, and then you'll have all the key components ready-set-go.

Select a main color and up to three accent colors.

No matter what the final design will be I first select a main color I want to design around and then no more than three accent colors. I think any more than three accent colors makes a piece look too busy. Of course, this is just my personal opinion, not the rule. Within each accent color, there are varying hues that you can use for blending.

The following are just some fail-safe color combinations I like: green and aqua, green and cranberry, purple and green, purple and teal, purple and cranberry, purple and blue, topaz and purple, green and topaz, cranberry and topaz, and turquoise and topaz. You will discover your favorite color combinations over time. Don't look too far or try too hard; your closet is the first stop for color hints. Even if you are designing for someone else, if you work with colors you like, your final design will "speak of you." Always make what you like first and foremost.

Add volume and dimension.

When selecting accent colors, I may twist stone strands together to see how they blend. What I am looking for is texture. I try not to find beads of the same shape for one piece, because you can achieve wonderful texture by varying the cut and size of the beads. You can add volume and dimension to your work by utilizing this concept.

Create visual texture.

To create visual texture besides using different shaped and sized beads, I select beads of varying hues in the same color family. For instance, if I am working with purple as the main color, I look into using lavender, lilac, amethyst, plum, magenta, or maroon as well.

Mix bead finishes and cuts.

The bead finish and cut are also important in creating visual textures. Don't select all faceted beads or Swarovski crystal components unless you want maximum glitz. I like to use faceted and unfaceted, shiny and matte, polished and unpolished beads in the same design. The matte, unpolished, and unfaceted beads balance the highlights.

Don't seek perfection.

Don't always feel that you have to buy the most expensive stone or component because some accent beads can be inexpensive. Slight imperfections, especially vintage beads and components, can add to your overall design and story. The main highlight should be the quality components, which will bring additional value to the finished design.

Stock favorite colors in two sizes.

Seed beads are relatively inexpensive. I prefer using Japanese seed beads for their uniformity and color range. I like a mix of the metallic, aurora borealis, luster, shimmering, and matte colors. Keep in stock colors you like in both size 11° and 15° (or sizes you prefer) and in shiny as well as matte versions if they are available. Matte color beads generally begin with an "F" prefix of the same color number. Metallic and matte seed beads are often more expensive due to additional processing at the factory, but because you don't use many accent beads, go ahead and splurge.

A little goes a long way.

There are also lovely small seed pearls, glass pearls, faceted metal beads, shaped Czech pressed-glass beads, and Swarovski crystals that can add small hints of textures. I like to stay within 2mm to 4mm in size. Just a small amount sprinkled throughout the design will do. A little goes a long way.

Avoid dyed stones.

If you want a natural look to your work, be wary of dyed stones. Some of the synthetic stones are actually glass. The colors are beautiful, but if you want to add value to your piece, make sure you shop at a reputable and knowledgeable vendor. If the price is too good, more than likely they are good "fakes". If you don't mind, then by all means purchase the bargain. Arm yourself with knowledge and get a good gemstone reference guide to educate yourself. The more you know, the less likely an unscrupulous vendor will attempt to take advantage of you.

Stitch a sample.

Make a sample swatch or string a mix of beads you want to use in a design. Look at the visual appeal. This is more of an exercise than a complete project. If you like the colors and mix, proceed forward. If it's not what you envision, go back to the drawing board and start over. Why invest in further time if you don't like the bead selection from the start? Many beads look different once blended with other beads. The more you design with similar color blends, the easier it will be to execute each subsequent design. Soon, choosing colors will be second nature.

Don't forget the finishing touches.

No matter how pretty your piece is in the front, it has to look equally pleasing in the back. The clasp is just as important as a design element. I usually pick a main accent color I want to feature. If I am purchasing a premade clasp, I like using clasps with inlaid faceted semiprecious gemstones, buttons, or vintage crystal stones to add richness and character to the overall look. A clasp may be so beautiful that you may want to make it the pendant. I collect turn-of-the-

century vintage buttons and often use them in my more intricate beadwork. Beads can also be transformed into innovative clasps. With beadweaving, a beaded button adds a seamless flow to the design. Basically, the sky's the limit as long as you maintain a good flow to the design.

Less is always more.

I have seen designs that are really pretty but are over embellished. Sometimes we can get carried away and don't know when to stop adding to a design. Unless you are making a showpiece for an exhibit or submission to a contest, think about wearability, practicality, and balance of design. Many showpieces are too heavy to wear and are only meant for display. Of course, beauty is in the eye of the beholder. What is pleasing to some may not be to another and vice versa.

IDEAS AND WHERE TO FIND INSPIRATION

Maybe I am lucky, but I see inspiration everywhere and in very ordinary things. I also have a vivid imagination. For instance, you may see a summer strap shoe but I see a beaded rope design.

Books

I also happen to be an information sponge with a voracious appetite for knowledge. I scour the Internet and research everything I do or design. I also LOVE reference books. This, of course, means that no art or jewelry book is safe from me. And like dessert, there is always room for just one more!

My books run the gamut of topics ranging from satellite and aerial photography to textiles and quilting. How's that for eclectic taste? These books are my most treasured possessions because they provide me with endless visual stimuli, flooding my mind with images that tease me to create.

You don't have to be a bibliophile to find inspiration. But if you want to start looking for books or magazines at the local bookstore or at your library, here are ten topics to get you started. And no, they are not all jewelry related.

Interior Design

Interior design books showcase how rooms are decorated. They help provide ideas on how to "set the mood" and create a theme for the colors you select to use in your piece.

Graphic and Ad Design

Ads have only a few seconds to catch your attention. Notice how graphic artists use color and images to their advantage.

Color Harmony Series

This is a series of color harmony books published by Rockport Publishers. I reference mine periodically when I want a color boost. I enjoy looking at the swatches of two or three colors that suggest ideas for harmonious color appeal. There are themes for natural, jewels, and pastel color palettes. The series also covers color harmony for digital photography and the Web.

Dover Publications

Dover is a great resource for copyright-free clip art, including nostalgic and ephemera images and motifs. Think beyond what you see in these books. For instance, I've used a nineteenth-century wrought-iron gate design and modified it to create a silver filigree bracelet.

Gardening, Flower, and Nature Photography

Nature is one of the best resources for inspiration. For example, study a close-up of a flower and see how colors variegate from one to the next. Look at an aerial or satellite photograph to see how to create texture and natural gradation in your work. I also love to look at animals, especially birds, for color harmony and inspiration.

Lighting and Furniture Catalogs

Furniture catalogs such as Crate & Barrel, Pottery Barn, and West Elm showcase textures and colors in beautiful room settings through textiles and decorative room accessories. Lighting designs also show interesting shapes that may be translated to jewelry designs.

Fashion and Accessories

While the runway has some quirky fashions and accessories, it gives you an idea of the seasonal color trends and styles. Use these as guidance, but don't lock yourself into following trends.

Textiles, Yarn, Fiber, and Quilting

Textiles and quilt books are great for color inspiration. Yarn and knitting designs can sometimes be translated into beadwork with some reengineering. What you can do with a crochet hook or knitting needles can be modified to work with beads and fibers. Hand-dyed textiles and fiber such as roving and yarn are a great source for color inspiration.

Jewelry History

They say styles come back en vogue every ten years. Knowing the history of jewelry designs can add a unique twist and story to your work. The history of the beads you use or the types of stones you select also adds new dimension to the finished design with a built-in, unique story.

Auction Catalogs

Jewelry and decorative art catalogs are great resources to learn about the history of jewelry. They contain beautiful photographs of private collections that would otherwise be unknown to the general public. The catalogs often provide a short history of the piece, the owner, the designer, and estimated values. Even if you can't afford one of these jewels, you can translate their inspiration by using more affordable beads and findings to make a design your own.

The Internet

With technology at our fingertips, the Internet is a great resource in finding free "eye candy". Here are some places you can seek free inspiration.

Facebook Common-Interest Groups: Join a beading or an art forum group on Facebook where like-minded artists share their art, resources, and advice. You will be exposed to many artists from many mediums from all over the world.

Pinterest: Pinterest is a pinboard-style photo-sharing site where users can create and manage folders of image collections that interest them. The pinboards can be shared with others. You can "like" and add comments just like with Facebook.

Google Image Searches: When you search for anything on Google, you can also search for images with the keyword. Google is the most powerful search engine in the world.

eBay: I am NOT buying; I am just looking. I especially seek out the antique, vintage, and collectible categories among the millions of listings. Just like an auction catalog, you can find some of the most unique items ever created by mankind.

Magazines and Catalogs

Another idea is to start clipping pages from magazines and catalogs that catch your eye. These images can contribute to a future design. I put these clippings in sheet protectors and then in a three-ring binder. Even though I may only go to this binder once in a while, I have a central place to thumb through for inspiration.

A Note about Copying

With all this being said and suggested, I'm not going to discuss the legalese of copyright laws, because we all should know right from wrong. This is especially the case if you are drawing inspiration from another artist's work. No matter where you get your ideas for your designs, be sure to make them your own. Just know that duplicating a design from a magazine to teach yourself a technique is one thing, but using the same design to replicate, teach, and sell is just darn wrong.

Many designers, teachers, and authors give a lot of themselves when sharing a design in the classroom or in a magazine or a book. They did all that hard work so you can benefit in learning. That is their gift to you without asking for much in return. Value that instead of disrespecting their art. Unfortunately, there are still unscrupulous people out there. The key to your own artistic growth is to challenge yourself to come up with new ideas, to take what you learn up a notch, and then when possible, to give back to the creative community.

CAPTURING YOUR VISION & CREATING YOUR ARTISTIC VOICE

The painter James McNeill Whistler's most commonly quoted quotation is "An artist is not paid for his labor but for his vision." How true is that? Payment is not necessarily monetary either, as there are many intangible rewards. As a novice, in the beginning, one naturally focuses on other's works. However, your personal artistic growth truly does not begin until you make a shift to find your own voice. Anyone can build skills to duplicate a design, but it is the visionary who has the authenticity of originality, taking intangible ideas and developing them into tangible creations. The visionary takes calculated risks, sometimes making mistakes, but keeps on treading forward to make things happen despite possible setbacks. No matter how long it takes, visionaries are persistent about achieving their goal to create that masterpiece.

Ideas come and go. I often carry a notepad and pen to document my thoughts and inspirations. Sometimes they are just short words or doodles that make no sense to anyone but me. These little bits of paper are priceless treasures that may lead to many possible grand designs. Some ideas are immediately explored while others may just "live on paper" until it's the right time. Some papers get lost or misplaced only to be found later to rejuvenate the original idea.

Tracking Your Ideas

Yes, ideas begin to have life when they are written down. And when you are ready to explore these ideas, they may undergo a metamorphosis and become much more than what you first imagined. It takes time to cultivate an idea. No one just sits down and creates wonderful works of art. There may actually be many instances where designs are created, taken apart, and re-created only to go back to the drawing board during the prototyping stage. If that's what it takes, that's what it takes. Don't finish a design if you are not happy with it during the creative process. It's better to start over. I know the dreaded words "start over" bothers and scares a lot of people. Rest and a good night's sleep sometimes bring new light to a dilemma or design challenge.

So when is a vision a good idea? When it is attempted and executed, even if it's not successful at first, it may grow into an even grander idea later. When is a vision a bad idea? When it is not attempted, thus never given the chance to develop or "live".

The Right Time

When inspiration strikes, you may not always have the time to immediately delve right in and explore. Some ideas may go unexplored or are forgotten temporarily to be revisited many days, months, and even years later. I don't think one necessarily has to rush into an idea without first planning the execution. I have a few ideas that took me several years to plan in my mind and then when it was finally the right time to execute, the design came together more quickly than without forethought. You will know when it's the right time. Perhaps you are one to just jump right in, design as you go, and wing it. There is a place and time for that also.

Try This

Let's go through an exercise. Look through any magazine with plenty of photos. Flip through and stop at the first ad that catches your eye. It may be the colors, the composition, the subject, the catch phrase, a company slogan, whatever that may have stopped you and said "look at me." Study this photo. In marketing and advertising, this is known as "branding," but I would like to refer to this as "telling a story" through words or images.

Telling Your Story

When you create what do you want to convey to your audience and what is the story you wish to tell them? Creating a piece of jewelry is very much like designing a clever ad because you want to capture the attention of the viewer. You can tell your story with the types of beads you select, evoke a certain mood with the color choices, create a theme by naming your piece, or perhaps add historical influences to the creation.

Artists desire to have a unique voice in their art medium. This can be viewed as the artist's style or "signature look". The artist likes to traverse off the beaten path and not follow trends or copy someone else's designs. The artist will wait until her/his art is ready to be completed with the right materials at the right time for that "perfect ending to a perfect story".

What inspires us to create? When you see a finished design at a show, in a magazine, in a book, or on a website, don't you admire the design or even critique it? It is natural to pick out elements you like and do not like. We are all critics. What may be pleasing to some may not be to another. There will always be the natural inclination for people to compare one artist to another. This can't be avoided, especially if their styles are similar. In the age of the Internet superhighway, information travels fast. We are constantly in a race to be the first to create the next fantabulous jewelry. It's not a race. Slow down and think about your artistic voice in your next creation.

BASIC TECHNIQUES

KNOTTING & WIREWORK

↓ Overhand Knot

Make a loop and pass the cord that lies behind the loop over the front cord and through the loop. Pull tight.

↓ Half-Hitch Knot

Half-hitch knots may be worked with two or more strands—one strand is knotted over one or more other strands. Form a loop around the cord(s). Pull the end through the loop just formed and pull tight **(A)**. Repeat for the length of cord you want to cover.

For half-hitch knots between beads, catch the thread from a previous pass and make an overhand knot, then weave through the next bead **(B)**.

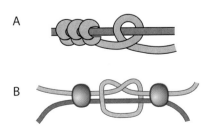

↓ Square Knot

The square knot is the classic sturdy knot for securing most stringing materials. First, make an overhand knot **(1)**, passing the right end **(blue thread)** over the left end **(red thread)**. Next, make another overhand knot **(2)**, this time passing the left end over the right end. Pull tight.

→ Wrapped Loop

Begin with a 90° bend at least 2" (5 cm) from the end of the wire. Use round-nose pliers to form a loop with a tail overlapping the bend. Wrap the tail tightly down the neck of the wire to create a couple of coils. Trim the excess wire to finish.

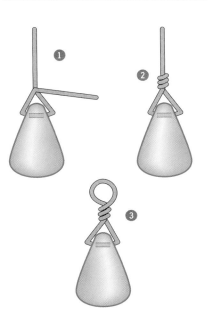

↑ Wrapped-Loop Bails

Wrapped-loop bails turn top-drilled beads, usually teardrops or briolettes, into pendants. Center the bead on a 3" (7.5 cm) or longer piece of wire **(1)**. Bend both ends of the wire up the sides and across the top of the bead. Bend one end straight up at the center of the bead **(2)**, then wrap the other wire around it to form a few coils. Form a wrapped loop with the straight-up wire, wrapping it back down over the already-formed coils **(3)**. Trim the excess wire.

BEADWEAVING

↓ Fringe

Exit from the foundation row bead or fabric **(1)**. String a length of beads plus one bead **(2)**. Skipping the last bead, pass back through all the beads just strung to form a fringe leg **(3)**. Pass back into the foundation row or fabric **(4)**.

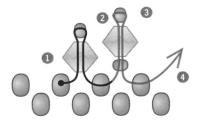

↓ Herringbone, Circular (Ndebele)

If there is an odd count, start **(1)**, then add one bead between each **(2)** and then two beads between each of those **(3)**. Increases generally occur in three rows of beading. Weave through one bead, string two beads, and weave down the adjacent bead. String one bead and up the second pair of two beads. Repeat around. On the next sequence, repeat but instead of stringing one bead, string two in between each pair of beads **(4)**. The third row of increases treats the two beads added as a pair of beads **(5)**. Next, weave a regular herringbone row in between each sequence of increases for a smoother transition.

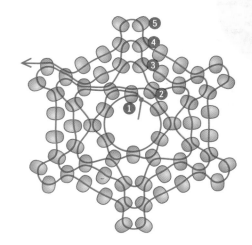

↓ Herringbone, Flat (Ndebele)

Begin with a foundation row of even-count ladder stitch. String two beads, pass down through the adjacent bead in the ladder and then up through the next bead. String two beads, pass down the next bead and then up through the bead after it. Repeat to the end of the row. To end the row, catch the thread from a previous round and then step up through the last bead strung (**blue thread**). To begin the next row, string two beads and pass down through the second bead of the previous row and up through the following bead. Repeat, stringing two beads per stitch and passing down the following bead (**red thread**). The two-bead stitch will cause the beads to angle up in each column, like a herringbone fabric.

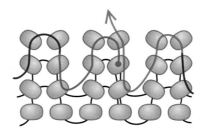

↑ Herringbone, Twisted Tubular

Begin with a foundation row of ladder stitch. Join the ends together to form a tube. String two beads. Pass down through the next bead and up through the bead after it. Repeat around the tube. At the end of the round, pass through the first beads of the previous and current rounds to step up. Repeat to round 3. To start the twist, string two beads—pass down through the next bead and up through the two previous rounds (**green thread**). Repeat around (**blue thread**). At the end of the round, pass up through the two previous rounds and the current round of three beads to step up to the new round (**red thread**). Repeat from *.

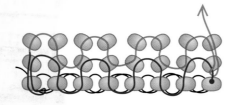

↓ Herringbone, Tubular

Begin with a foundation row of ladder stitch. Join the ends together to form a tube (**blue thread**). String two beads. Pass down through the next bead and up through the bead after it. Repeat around the tube. At the end of the round, pass through the first beads of the previous and current rounds to step up to the new round (**red thread**).

↑ Ladder Stitch

Thread a needle on each end of the thread and pass one needle through one or more beads from left to right and pass the other needle through the same beads from right to left. Continue adding beads by crisscrossing both needles through one bead at a time. Use this stitch to make strings of beads or as the foundation for brick or herringbone stitch.

To work a single-needle ladder stitch, string two beads and pass through them again (**blue thread**). String one bead. Pass through the last stitched bead and the one just strung. Repeat, adding one bead at a time and working in a figure-eight pattern (**red thread**).

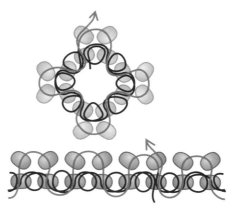

↓ Netting (Single Needle)

Begin by stringing a base row of thirteen beads **(1)**. String five beads and go back through the fifth bead from the end of the base row **(2)**. String another five beads, skip three beads of the base row, and go back through the next; repeat to the end of the row. To turn, pass back through the last three beads (one leg of the last net) **(3)**. String five beads, pass back through the center bead of the next net, and continue **(4)**.

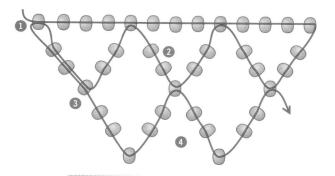

↓ Peyote Stitch, Circular

String three beads and form the first round by passing through the first bead **(green thread)**. For the second round, string two beads and pass through the next bead of the previous round; repeat twice **(blue thread)**. To step up for the next round, pass through the first bead of the current round. For the third round, string one bead and pass through the next bead of the previous round; repeat all around, then step up at the end of the round **(red thread)**. Continue in this manner, alternating the two rounds. You may need to adjust the bead count depending upon the relative size of the beads in order to keep the circle flat.

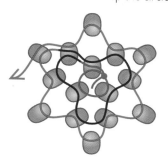

↓ Peyote Stitch, Decreasing

To make a mid-project decrease, simply pass thread through two beads without adding a bead in the "gap" **(blue thread)**. In the next row, work a regular one-drop peyote over the decrease **(red thread)**. Keep tension taut to avoid holes.

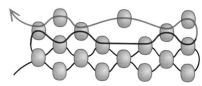

↓ Peyote Stitch, Flat Even

One-drop peyote stitch begins by stringing an even number of beads to create the first two rows. Begin the third row by stringing one bead **(blue thread)** and passing through the second-to-last bead of the previous rows. String another bead and pass through the fourth-to-last bead of the previous rows. Continue adding one bead at a time, passing over every other bead of the previous rows **(red thread)**.

↓ Two-Drop Peyote Stitch

is worked the same as above but with two beads at a time instead of one.

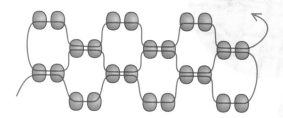

↓ Peyote Stitch, Tubular Even Count

For even-count tubular peyote stitch, string an even number of beads and knot the tail and working threads to form the first two rounds; pass through the first two beads strung **(blue thread)**. To work round 3, string one bead, skip one bead, and pass through the next bead; repeat around until you have added half the number of beads in the first round. Step up through the first bead added in this round **(red thread)**.

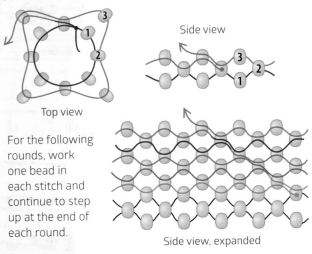

Top view

Side view

Side view, expanded

For the following rounds, work one bead in each stitch and continue to step up at the end of each round.

↓ Picot

To make a picot, string three **(A)** or five **(B)** beads and weave into the next high bead. This sequence is woven into the gaps of edge beading to create a lacy effect and is sometimes used to transition to decreasing stitches or serve as connection points.

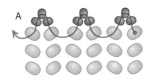

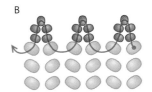

↓ Reverse Picot

To make a reverse picot, string three beads **(A)** or five beads **(B)** and weave into the opposite end of the same high bead just exited, then down the bead adjoining two adjacent high beads, so that the thread does not show. Reverse picots are also described as right-angle-weave links.

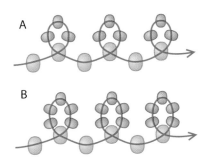

An alternate version **(C)** is to hide the gap between two reverse picots by weaving a bead in between.

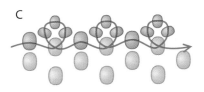

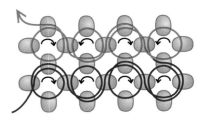

↑ Right-Angle Weave (Single Needle)

String four beads and pass through the first two beads again to form the first unit. For the rest of the row, string three beads, then pass through the last bead passed through in the previous unit and the first two just strung; the thread path will resemble a figure eight, alternating directions with each unit **(blue thread)**. To begin the next row, pass through beads to exit the side of the last unit. String three beads, then pass through the original side bead of the previous row and the first bead just strung. *String two beads, pass through the next edge bead of the previous row, the last bead passed through in the previous unit, and the last two beads just strung. Pass through the next edge bead of the previous row, string two beads, then pass through the last bead of the previous unit, the edge bead just passed through, and the first bead just strung **(red thread)**. Repeat from * to complete the row, then begin a new row as before.

↓ Right-Angle Weave, Circular

Circular right-angle weave begins like tubular right-angle weave with a change in size or number of beads added to the top edge. The bead size and quantity of beads added in successive rounds flattens the original tube into a circle.

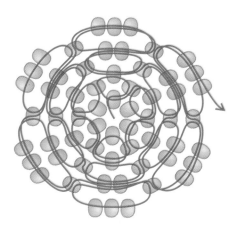

→ Right-Angle Weave, Cubic

Cubic right-angle weave is the same as tubular right-angle weave but with generally only four units, which creates six faces (or walls) to form a cube. On the last wall, circle around the beadwork to reinforce before continuing building length.

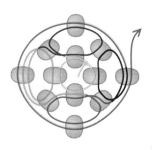

↓ Right-Angle Weave, Tubular

Create a flat strip of right-angle weave with one less unit than the desired circumference. Connect the last stitch to the first stitch. Exit the end bead of the last round, string a bead, and pass through the first bead of the first unit. String another bead and pass through the bead of the last stitch to complete this unit **(red thread)**. To begin the next round, pass through the beads to exit from a bead on the top edge. String three beads. Pass through the original bead, the three beads just strung, and the top bead of the previous round. *String two beads. Pass through side bead of the previous unit, the original top bead where your thread is exiting, and the next top bead of the previous round. Repeat from * until there is one uncompleted stitch. Depending on the amount of repeats, the thread is either exiting up or down the side bead of the last unit. String one bead. If the thread path is facing up, **pass through the side bead of the first unit, the top bead of the previous round, the side bead of the last unit, and the bead just strung.. Then begin a new round as before. If the thread is facing down, ***pass through the top bead of the last stitch in the previous round and up through the side bead of the first unit of the current round. String one bead. Pass through the side bead of the last unit, repeat from *** and pass through the bead just strung. Then begin a new round as before.

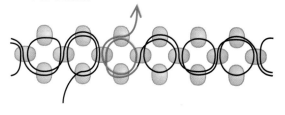

↓ Scallop Edging

Scallop edging is overlapping loop fringe created to decorate a peyote or right-angle-weave edge. From an edge bead, *string any number of beads, skip a bead, and pass through the next bead in the opposite direction. String a bead and weave into the skipped bead. Repeat from *.

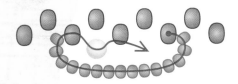

↓ Square Stitch, Circular

For circular square stitch, string the first round of beads and pass through them again to form a circle. Start a new round by stringing two beads; pass through the last bead of the first round and through the two beads just strung. Repeat around, passing through the next bead of the previous round for each two new beads strung. At the end of the round, pass through the whole round again to tighten the beads. Start a new round by stringing two beads; pass through the last bead of the previous round and through the two beads just strung. String one bead and pass through the next bead of the previous round and the bead just strung. Repeat around, stringing one or two beads to each bead of the previous round, adjusting the count as necessary to keep the work flat.

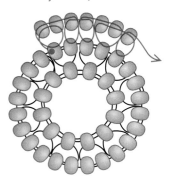

↓ Square Stitch, Flat

Begin by stringing a row of beads (blue thread). For the second row, string one bead, then pass through the last bead of the first row and back through the bead just strung. Continue by stringing one bead and then passing through the second-to-last bead of the first row and back through the bead just strung. Repeat this looping technique to the end of the row (red thread).

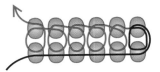

To make a decrease, weave thread through the previous row and exit from the bead adjacent to the place where you want to decrease. Continue working in square stitch.

To make an increase, string the number of beads at the end of the row where you want to increase. Work the next row the same as the previous row.

↓ St. Petersburg Chain

(A) Attach a stop bead. String 4A, then pass back through the first and second A beads, creating a ladder stitch. Pull to align the beads side by side (orange thread). String 1B (core bead) and pass back through the second and first A beads, then up through the fourth and third As (green thread). *String 4A and then pass through the first and second A beads just strung (blue thread). String 1B and pass back through the second and first beads of the 4A beads just added and through the third A bead from the first set of 4A beads. String 1C and pass through the third and fourth A beads from this step. Repeat from * to desired length. The second diagram (B) shows how to add a double St. Petersburg chain through a common core bead (B).

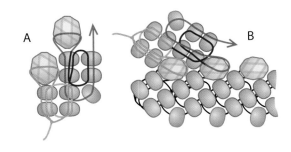

↓ Stitch-in-the-Ditch Embellishment

The stitch in the ditch is performed on top of an existing layer of peyote. Exit the beadwork from the original layer. *String the beads called for in the pattern and pass through the next bead on the same row of the original peyote layer. Repeat from *.

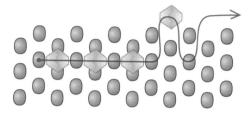

↓ Zipping

Two edges of peyote stitch can be zipped together by passing from an up bead on one side of the beadwork **(1)** to the up bead on the opposite side of beadwork **(2)**, interlocking the edges together like a zipper.

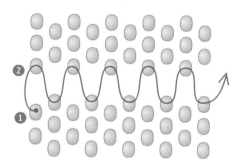

BEAD EMBROIDERY
↓ Backstitch

Tie a knot at the end of the thread. Pass up through the foundation from back to front. String two beads and lay them against the foundation. Pass down through the foundation next to the second bead, up through the front of the first bead, and then through both beads **(blue thread)**. *String two beads and pass down through the foundation next to the last bead just strung. Pass up through the foundation between the first and second beads and then through the second, third, and fourth beads **(red thread)**. Repeat from *.

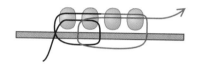

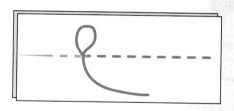

↑ Running Stitch or Straight Stitch

The stitch is worked by passing the needle in and out of the fabric to hold two or more layers together. The stitches may be of varying lengths, but the shorter the length, the sturdier the attachment. Typically, there is more thread visible on the top of the sewing than on the underside.

PROJECT RESOURCES

Many of the materials used in *Bead Metamorphosis* can be found at your local bead shop or contact the companies listed here. I've provided the seed bead color numbers for each project in the main colorways. If a bead or finding is no longer available, there are always suitable substitutes. You may also contact me at LisaKanDesigns@yahoo.com if you have any difficulty locating materials.

AUDREY FRINGE BRACELET, PAGE 32: CzechMate bricks and lentils: Aria Design Studio. Swarovski pearls and bicones: Fire Mountain Gems and Beads. Seed beads (Toho 990 and Miyuki 457L/457G): Out on a Whim or Bobby Beads. FireLine: Cabela's.

BELLA FIORE, PAGE 102: Silk ribbons and silk ties: Textile Geisha. Swarovski bicones and pearls: Fire Mountain Gems and Beads. Seed beads (Toho 221, 989; Miyuki 375A): Out on a Whim or Bobby Beads. FireLine: Cabela's.

CATHERINE BRACELET, PAGE 80: Super-Duos and Swarovski sliders: Aria Design Studio. Swarovski pearls, crystal bicones, and slider clasp: Fire Mountain Gems and Beads. Seed beads (Toho 221 and Miyuki 377L): Out on a Whim or Bobby Beads. FireLine: Cabela's.

CATHERINE NECKLACE, PAGE 86: Super-Duos: Aria Design Studio. Swarovski pearls, drops, rhinestones, and slider clasp: Fire Mountain Gems and Beads. Seed beads (Toho 83, 85, 221; Miyuki 377L): Out on a Whim, Starman, Inc., or Bobby Beads. FireLine: Cabela's.

CHRYSANTHEMUM BROOCH, PAGE 44: Rizos, daggers, and pin brooch: Aria Design Studio. Pin back brooch converter, double-sided tape, and rivoli rhinestone: Fire Mountain Gems and Beads. Seed beads (Miyuki 301, 457L/457G): Out on a Whim. FireLine: Cabela's.

CROWN JEWELS EARRINGS, PAGE 98: Swarovski bicones, pearls, and ear wires: Fire Mountain Gems and Beads. Seed beads (Toho 221, 989): Starman, Inc. or Bobby Beads. Chain: Rio Grande. FireLine: Cabela's.

CROWN JEWELS NECKLACE, PAGE 118: Swarovski sliders: Aria Design Studio. Swarovski bicones, round pearls, and drop pearls: Fire Mountain Gems and Beads. Seed beads (Toho 221, 989): Starman, Inc. or Bobby Beads. Dritz sew-on snaps: Jo-Ann Fabric and Craft. FireLine: Cabela's.

DECO CHANDELIER EARRINGS, PAGE 16: CzechMate 2-hole bricks: Aria Design Studio. Swarovski pearls and bicones: Fire Mountain Gems and Beads. Seed beads (Toho 221, 327): Starman, Inc. or Bobby Beads. Chain, wire, and ear wires: Rio Grande. FireLine: Cabela's.

DECO LACE BRACELET, PAGE 20: CzechMate 2-hole bricks: Aria Design Studio. Swarovski pearls and bicones: Fire Mountain Gems and Beads. Seed beads (Toho 221, 321, 327): Starman, Inc. or Bobby Beads. Dritz sew-on snaps: Jo-Ann Fabric and Craft. FireLine: Cabela's.

ENCANTO, PAGE 130: 2mm Czech pearls, fire-polished glass rounds, and Rulla beads: Aria Design Studio. Swarovski pearls and barrel clasp: Fire Mountain Gems and Beads. Custom-coated rivoli rhinestones: EH Ashley. Seed beads (Toho 90, 166B, 221, 321; Miyuki F460G, F460H, F460Q): Out on a Whim, Starman, Inc., or Bobby Beads. FireLine: Cabela's. No-Tangle bobbin: Jo-Ann Fabric and Craft.

HANAMI, PAGE 110: 2mm Czech pearls, pin back, and shibori hand-dyed silk ribbons: Aria Design Studio. Silk ties: Textile Geisha. Swarovski rivolis: Fire Mountain Gems and Beads. Seed beads (Toho 221; Miyuki 301, 375A): Out on a Whim or Bobby Beads. FireLine: Cabela's. Olfa rotary cutter and self-healing mat: Jo-Ann Fabric and Craft.

ISADORA EARRINGS, PAGE 26: Czech-Mate triangles, chain, and Preciosa drops: Aria Design Studio. Swarovski pearls: Fire Mountain Gems and Beads. Ear wires and gauged wire: Rio Grande. Seed beads (Toho 83, 221): Starman, Inc. FireLine: Cabela's.

KAYLA LARIAT, PAGE 62: 2mm Czech pearls, Rizos, fire-polished rounds, and cord: Aria Design Studio. Swarovski pearls and rivolis: Fire Mountain Gems and Beads. Seed beads (Toho, 224, 327, 410C, 460A, 928): Out on a Whim, Bobby Beads, or Starman, Inc. FireLine: Cabela's.

RIVOLI SCALLOP CHAIN EARRINGS, PAGE 40: Rivolis: Fire Mountain Gems and Beads. Ear wires: Rio Grande. Seed beads (Miyuki 301, 457L/457G): Out on a Whim. FireLine: Cabela's.

SUNDARA, PAGE 50: 2mm Czech pearls and fire-polished beads: Aria Design Studio. Rivolis and rhinestone drop: Fire Mountain Gems and Beads. Seed beads (Toho 459, 221): Bobby Beads or Starman, Inc. Dritz snap and No-Tangle bobbin: Jo-Ann Fabric and Craft. FireLine: Cabela's.

TREFOIL EARRINGS, PAGE 74: Super-Duos: Aria Design Studio. Swarovski pearls, crystal bicones, and drops: Fire Mountain Gems and Beads. Ear wires: Rio Grande. Seed beads (Toho 321, 711): Starman, Inc. or Bobby Beads. FireLine: Cabela's.

WHERE TO SHOP

ARIA DESIGN STUDIO
PO Box 820494
Vancouver, WA 98682
ariadesignstudio.com

BOBBY BEADS
2831 Hennepin Ave. S.
Minneapolis, MN 55408
(888) 900-2323
bobbybead.com

CABELA'S
(800) 237-4444
cabelas.com

EH ASHLEY
(wholesale only)
1 White Squadron Rd.
Riverside, RI 02915
(800) 735-7424
ehashley.com

FIRE MOUNTAIN GEMS AND BEADS
1 Fire Mountain Wy.
Grants Pass, OR 97526
(800) 355-2137
firemountaingems.com

JO-ANN FABRIC AND CRAFT STORES
(888) 739-4120
joann.com

OUT ON A WHIM
121 E. Cotati Ave.
Cotati, CA 94931
(800) 232-3111
www.whimbeads.com

RIO GRANDE
7500 Bluewater Rd. NW
Albuquerque, NM 87121
(800) 545-6566
riogrande.com

STARMAN, INC.
(wholesale only)
250 Center Park Wy.
Sequim, WA 98382
(888) 683-2323
starmaninc.com

TEXTILE GEISHA
PO Box 820494
Vancouver, WA 98682
textilegeisha.com